Investing in strategies to reverse the global incidence of TB

Lead authors
Jaap Broekmans, Coordinator
Karen Caines
Joan E. Paluzzi

UN Millennium Project
Task Force on HIV/AIDS, Malaria, TB, and
Access to Essential Medicines
Working Group on TB
2005

London • Sterling, Va.

First published by Earthscan in the UK and USA in 2005

Reprinted 2005
Copyright © 2005
by the United Nations Development Programme
All rights reserved

ISBN: 1-84407-223-1 paperback

For a full list of publications please contact:

Earthscan
8–12 Camden High Street
London, NW1 0JH, UK
Tel: +44 (0)20 7387 8558
Fax: +44 (0)20 7387 8998
Email: earthinfo@earthscan.co.uk
Web: www.earthscan.co.uk

22883 Quicksilver Drive, Sterling, VA 20166-2012, USA

Earthscan is an imprint of James and James (Science Publishers) Ltd and publishes in association with the International Institute for Environment and Development

A catalogue record for this book is available from the British Library

Library of Congress Cataloging-in-Publication Data

A catalog record has been requested

This report should be cited as UN Millennium Project 2005. *Investing in strategies to reverse the global incidence of TB.* Task Force on HIV/AIDS, Malaria, TB, and Access to Essential Medicines.

Photos: Front cover Jørgen Schytte/UNDP; back cover, top to bottom, Christopher Dowswell, Pedro Cote/UNDP, Giacomo Pirozzi/Panos Pictures, Liba Taylor/Panos Pictures, Jørgen Schytte/UNDP, UN Photo Library, Giacomo Pirozzi/UNICEF, Curt Carnemark/World Bank, Pedro Cote/UNDP, Franck Charton/UNICEF, Paul Chesley/Getty Images, Ray Witlin/World Bank, Pete Turner/Getty Images.

This book was edited, designed, and produced by Communications Development Inc., Washington, D.C., and its UK design partner, Grundy & Northedge.

The Millennium Project was commissioned by the UN Secretary-General and sponsored by the UN Development Group, which is chaired by the Administrator of the United Nations Development Programme. The report is an independent publication that reflects the views of the members of the Task Force on HIV/AIDS, Malaria, TB, and Access to Essential Medicines, Working Group on TB, who contributed in their personal capacity. This publication does not necessarily reflect the views of the United Nations, the United Nations Development Programme, or their Member States.

Printed in Malta by Gutenberg Press on elemental chlorine-free paper

Foreword

The world has an unprecedented opportunity to improve the lives of billions of people by adopting practical approaches to meeting the Millennium Development Goals. At the request of UN Secretary-General Kofi Annan, the UN Millennium Project has identified practical strategies to eradicate poverty by scaling up investments in infrastructure and human capital while promoting gender equality and environmental sustainability. These strategies are described in the UN Millennium Project's report *Investing in Development: A Practical Plan to Achieve the Millennium Development Goals*, which was coauthored by the coordinators of the UN Millennium Project task forces.

The task forces have identified the interventions and policy measures needed to achieve each of the Goals. In *Investing in Strategies to Reverse the Global Incidence of TB*, the Working Group on TB of the Task Force on HIV/ AIDS, Malaria, TB, and Access to Essential Medicines addresses the devastating impact of TB on both human health and economic performance. TB can be controlled. Transmission of TB and deaths due to the disease can be reduced dramatically through known and proven interventions. Yet because these interventions are not applied as widely as they need to be, millions of people die each year of TB and millions more are incapacitated. This report provides concrete and practical steps that governments and international agencies can take to treat and prevent this illness.

The members of the Working Group on TB have brought an impressive body of individual experience and expertise to this effort. They have contributed in their personal capacity and volunteered their time to this important task. Many members have in addition been key contributors to the Global Partnership to Stop TB's coordinated and global effort against the disease. I am grateful for their thorough and skilled work, and I am sure that the practical recommendations for action in this report will make an important

contribution to achieving the Millennium Development Goals. I strongly recommend this report to all who are fighting against extreme poverty and disease. It will help readers everywhere to understand how much more we can
accomplish.

Jeffrey D. Sachs
New York
January 17, 2005

Contents

Boxes

Figures

Maps

Tables

Working group members

Task force coordinator

Jaap Broekmans, Director, KNCV Tuberculosis Foundation

Members of the Working Group on TB

Nils Billo, Executive Director, International Union Against Tuberculosis and Lung Disease

Ken Castro, Assistant Surgeon General, U.S. Public Health Service, Director, Division of Tuberculosis Elimination, National Center for HIV, STD, and TB Prevention, Centers for Disease Control and Prevention

Marcos Espinal, Executive Secretary, Stop TB Partnership, World Health Organization

Katherine Floyd, Health Economist, Stop TB Department, World Health Organization

Anthony Harries, Malawi Community Health Sciences Unit

Philip Hopewell, University of California, San Francisco at San Francisco General Hospital

Dermot Maher, Medical Officer, Stop TB Department, World Health Organization

P.R. Narayanan, Director, Tuberculosis Research Centre Chetput-Chennai, India

Mikhail Perelman, Director, Research Institute of Phthisio-pulmonology, I.M. Sechenov Moscow Medicine Academy

Mario Raviglione, Director, Stop TB Department, World Health Organization

Nina Schwalbe, Senior Fellow, International Health, Open Society Institute

Roberto Tapia-Conyer, Subsecretaría de Prevención y Promoción de la Salud, Mexico

Diana Weil, formerly Senior Public Health Specialist, Health, Nutrition and Population Team, World Bank; currently Senior Policy Adviser, Stop TB Department, World Health Organization

Task force associate

Joan E. Paluzzi, Partners In Health

Preface

The UN Millennium Project was commissioned in 2002 by the United Nations Secretary-General, Kofi Annan, to recommend the best strategies for achieving the Millennium Development Goals. Its task—mainly undertaken by 10 thematically orientated task forces—is to identify the operational priorities, organizational means of implementation, and financing structures necessary to achieve the Goals.

This report recommends an operational framework of action to meet the targets for tuberculosis (TB): to halve the prevalence of TB disease and deaths between 1990 and 2015. It is the work of the UN Millennium Project Working Group on TB, which operates within the UN Millennium Project's Task Force on HIV/AIDS, Malaria, TB, and Access to Essential Medicines.

Millions of people, most of them (not coincidentally) living in profound poverty, die of TB each year. Many more will be acutely sick and debilitated. This correlation between TB and the impact of poverty on men, women, and children highlights the importance of a multifaceted approach to resolving the devastating problems facing the most vulnerable members of the global community in the twenty-first century.

The membership of the Working Group on TB includes independent experts drawn from the public sector, civil society organizations, academia, and UN agencies. The report is based on the working group's own research and a broad range of inputs and documents, including those from national TB programs, operational research, international agencies, and journals.

Acknowledgments

The UN Millennium Project Working Group on TB, led by Task Force Coordinator Jaap Broekmans, is indebted to a wide range of partners for their assistance in preparing this report.

We should like to express our thanks to the writing committee of Jaap Broekmans, Dermot Maher, Mario Raviglione, Nina Schwalbe, and Diana Weil who reviewed the document in process and provided guidance and contributions. Margaret Kruk and other colleagues in the UN Millennium Project secretariat provided invaluable advice and support. Our thanks also to Jim Kim for his leadership in the first year of the Project.

Task force members who were able to attend our meetings in Geneva and New Delhi provided valuable guidance and support. We sincerely thank Nils Billo, Ken Castro, Marcos Espinal, Philip Hopewell, and P.R. Narayanan. We are also grateful to Maria Freire, Gwynne Osterbaan, Sarah England, and Francesca Boldrini who joined us as guests at the New Delhi meeting and provided important feedback. We sincerely thank Barry Bloom for his contribution to the work of the working group during the first year of the project.

We are particularly grateful to contributors to this report. These include Lisa Adams of Dartmouth Medical School and Christy Hanson of PATH for the Kenya case study; Wayne Getz of the University at California at Berkeley, Josh Salomon of Harvard University, Martien Bergdorff, and Frank Cobelens of the KNCV Tuberculosis Foundation, and Gwynne Oosterbaan and Joelle Tanguy of the Global Alliance for TB Drug Development for the modeling study on the impact of new TB drugs; Anthony Harries for his contribution on operational research; Winstone Zulu of the Kara Counseling and Training Trust; Lorraine Mkabela and Lettie Longwe of AMARC Africa; and Partners In Health interns Ben Powers, Kashif Khan, and Kate Gregg for research and development of the country case studies on Cambodia, the Dominican Republic, and Ethiopia.

The working group also wishes to thank the World Health Organization (WHO) for use of data and findings from its Global TB Monitoring and Surveillance Project, which form the basis of the section on the status of the TB epidemic and TB control, and to WHO and the International Union Against TB and Lung Disease (IUATLD) for use of findings from their Global Project on Anti-tuberculosis Drug Resistance Surveillance.

Muhwa Jeremiah Chakaya, Marcos Espinal, Jose Figueroa Munoz, Malgosia Grzemska, Pieter Johannes, René L'Herminez, Pierre-Yves Norval, Jayavanth Pratap, Fabio Scano, and Jan van den Hombergh provided valued suggestions on the country case studies. Other parts of the report benefited from the advice and contributions of Leo Blanc, Francesca Boldrini, Joanne Carter, Chris Dye, Sarah England, Katherine Floyd, Lawrence J. Geiter, Rachel Guglielmo, Mark Harrington, Petra Heitkamp, Ernest Jaramillo, Suzanna Pak, Alasdair Reid, Giorgio Roscigno, Catherine Watts, and Natalie S. Waugh. Our thanks go to all.

The report was edited and produced by Meta de Coquereaumont, Mary Goundrey, Betsy Kulamer, Bruce Ross-Larson, Hope Steele, Christopher Trott, and Elaine Wilson of Communications Development Incorporated.

Partners In Health in Boston has served as the secretariat. We thank them for the logistical and administrative support they have provided to this working group. We also gratefully acknowledge the additional support provided to this task force working group by the Open Society Institute.

Abbreviations

Aeras	Aeras Global TB Vaccine Foundation
AIDS	acquired immunodeficiency syndrome
BCG	Bacillus Camille Guerin (vaccine)
DOTS	internationally recommended control strategy for tuberculosis
EPI	Expanded Program on Immunizations
FIND	Foundation for Innovative New Diagnostics
GDEP	Global DOTS Expansion Plan
GDF	Global Drug Facility
GFATM	Global Fund to Fight AIDS, Tuberculosis and Malaria
GLC	Green Light Committee
HIV	human immunodeficiency virus
IUATLD	International Union Against Tuberculosis and Lung Disease
KNCV	KNCV Tuberculosis Foundation
MDR-TB	multidrug-resistant tuberculosis
NGO	nongovernmental organization
NTP	National Tuberculosis Program
R&D	research and development
SS+	sputum smear positive
TB	tuberculosis
TB Alliance	Global Alliance for TB Drug Development
TB/HIV	co-infection with human immunodeficiency virus and tuberculosis
TLCP	Tuberculosis and Leprosy Control Program
UNDP	United Nations Development Programme
USAID	United States Agency for International Development
WHO	World Health Organization

Millennium Development Goals

Goal 1

Eradicate extreme poverty and hunger

Target 1.
Halve, between 1990 and 2015, the proportion of people whose income is less than $1 a day

Target 2.
Halve, between 1990 and 2015, the proportion of people who suffer from hunger

Goal 2

Achieve universal primary education

Target 3.
Ensure that, by 2015, children everywhere, boys and girls alike, will be able to complete a full course of primary schooling

Goal 3

Promote gender equality and empower women

Target 4.
Eliminate gender disparity in primary and secondary education, preferably by 2005, and in all levels of education no later than 2015

Goal 4

Reduce child mortality

Target 5.
Reduce by two-thirds, between 1990 and 2015, the under-five mortality rate

Goal 5

Improve maternal health

Target 6.
Reduce by three-quarters, between 1990 and 2015, the maternal mortality ratio

Goal 6

Combat HIV/AIDS, malaria, and other diseases

Target 7.
Have halted by 2015 and begun to reverse the spread of HIV/AIDS

Target 8.
Have halted by 2015 and begun to reverse the incidence of malaria and other major diseases

Goal 7

Ensure environmental sustainability

Target 9.
Integrate the principles of sustainable development into country policies and programs and reverse the loss of environmental resources

Target 10.
Halve, by 2015, the proportion of people without sustainable access to safe drinking water and basic sanitation

Target 11.
Have achieved by 2020 a significant improvement in the lives of at least 100 million slum dwellers

Goal 8

Develop a global partnership for development

Target 12.
Develop further an open, rule-based, predictable, nondiscriminatory trading and financial system (includes a commitment to good governance, development, and poverty reduction—both nationally and internationally)

Target 13.
Address the special needs of the Least Developed Countries (includes tariff- and quota-free access for Least Developed Countries' exports, enhanced program of debt relief for heavily indebted poor countries [HIPCs] and cancellation of official bilateral debt, and more generous official development assistance for countries committed to poverty reduction)

Target 14.
Address the special needs of landlocked developing countries and small island developing states (through the Program of Action for the Sustainable Development of Small Island Developing States and 22nd General Assembly provisions)

Target 15.
Deal comprehensively with the debt problems of developing countries through national and international measures in order to make debt sustainable in the long term

Target 16.
In cooperation with developing countries, develop and implement strategies for decent and productive work for youth

Target 17.
In cooperation with pharmaceutical companies, provide access to affordable essential drugs in developing countries

Target 18.
In cooperation with the private sector, make available the benefits of new technologies, especially information and communications technologies

Executive summary

I am living proof that TB can be beaten. With treatment, TB patients can be cured; TB untreated is life-threatening. Share the responsibility and share the reward of knowing you are saving lives. Every breath does count, so stop TB now and let people live!

—Archbishop Desmond Tutu, Nobel Laureate
(Second Stop TB Partners' Forum, March 2004)

Tuberculosis—A global health emergency

Tuberculosis (TB) causes 2 million deaths and unquantifiable suffering each year, despite the fact that proven, cost-effective treatments have been available for decades.

Over 10 years ago, the World Health Organization (WHO) declared TB a global health emergency. It is still an emergency today. Globally, TB rates continue to rise. TB is one of the world's leading causes of death and of the global burden of disease. It is a major killer of women, rivaling maternal mortality. It is a prime cause of death in people with HIV. Children are particularly vulnerable to TB infection as they are often held close and breathed on.

One-third of the world's population is latently infected with the bacillus that causes TB (*Mycobacterium tuberculosis*), though most will show no symptoms. Although only a small proportion of these people will develop active TB, the sheer scale of the full disease is startling. In 2002, there were nearly 9 million new cases of TB. Each person with active TB will infect 10–15 people every year on average.

TB afflicts the poor above all. Airborne mycobacteria spread easily in over-crowded places and where other illnesses and poor nutrition reduce people's immune defenses. Ninety-five percent of all TB sufferers live in developing countries. Most are poor people ages 15–54, who should be in their

Poverty, HIV, and deadly multidrug-resistant tuberculosis strains are key drivers of the TB epidemic

prime productive and reproductive years. Too often TB traps patients and their families in a cycle of disease and impoverishment. And the stigma of TB disrupts the social fabric of society.

Poverty, HIV, and deadly multidrug-resistant tuberculosis (MDR-TB) strains are key drivers of the TB epidemic. Their impact is evident in the huge variations in TB incidence around the world. The worst affected countries are in Sub-Saharan Africa, parts of Asia, and countries within Eastern Europe. In some regions, the rate for cases reported to WHO has been roughly stable or in decline. But it has been rising quickly in African countries with high HIV prevalence (7 percent per year, 1997–2002), and in Eastern Europe—mainly the former Soviet Union (5 percent per year) where drug resistance is a factor—compounded by collapse of the public health system and socioeconomic distress.

Urgent action is needed.

Halve tuberculosis prevalence and deaths by 2015

The Millennium Development target for TB is to have halted and begun to reverse its incidence by 2015 (box 1). To provide a measurable target, the Working Group on TB of the UN Millennium Project Task Force on HIV/AIDS, Malaria, TB, and Access to Essential Medicines recommends that the global TB control target should be to halve the prevalence of TB disease and deaths between 1990 and 2015. These targets are demanding but achievable. This report shows how.

The context for action is the full set of Millennium Development Goals (see Goals on p. xviii). They provide a crucial framework for helping reverse the TB epidemic, linking TB control to overall health sector development and development activities in general. Action taken to meet the target for TB will both contribute to and benefit from action taken to meet the other Millennium Development Goals targets, particularly those targeting poverty, gender issues, HIV/AIDS, and access to essential medicines.

Current tuberculosis control: scaling up the DOTS strategy

Effective TB control depends on the rapid identification and cure of infectious cases. The good news is that the internationally recognized strategy for

Box 1
Millennium Development Goal, target, and indicators for tuberculosis

Millennium Development Goal 6: Combat HIV/AIDS, malaria, and other diseases
Target 8: Have halted by 2015 and begun to reverse the incidence of malaria and other major diseases
Indicator 23: Prevalence and death rates associated with tuberculosis
Indicator 24: Proportion of tuberculosis cases detected and cured under DOTS (internationally recommended tuberculosis control strategy)
Recommended tuberculosis control target: to halve prevalence of tuberculosis disease and deaths between 1990 and 2015.

DOTS has proven remarkably effective

TB treatment—DOTS—has proven remarkably effective. Since 1995, over 13 million TB patients have been treated under DOTS. Out of 210 countries, 180 are implementing the strategy. Recent statistics from China—one of the countries most affected by the TB epidemic—suggest that DOTS implementation led to a 30 percent reduction of TB prevalence and improved treatment rates in just seven years.

The Stop TB Partnership, a global alliance of organizations engaged in TB control efforts established in 2001, has already registered significant progress in improving access to drugs through its Global Drug Facility (GDF) for anti-TB drugs and Green Light Committee for drug-resistant TB; mobilizing increased international support and resource flows for TB control (including through collaboration with the Global Fund to Fight AIDS, Tuberculosis, and Malaria); coordinating technical assistance; promoting approaches to control HIV-related TB and MDR-TB; and helping to develop new diagnostics, drugs, and vaccines.

The World Health Assembly has set process targets for 2005 of detecting 70 percent of new infectious cases of TB and successfully treating 85 percent of those detected. Achieving these twin targets under DOTS should be sufficient to halt the incidence of TB in all countries (including those with high rates of multidrug resistance), except countries with high rates of HIV infection.

The bad news is that some of the world's poorest and most TB-stricken communities do not yet have access to DOTS, despite global support for its implementation. And even where DOTS programs are theoretically available, not all TB patients can actually access them—because of the barriers created by poverty, physical isolation, and entrenched social practices.

In 2002 only 37 percent of the estimated number of smear-positive TB cases were captured by DOTS programs—little more than halfway to next year's World Health Assembly target of 70 percent. Recent signs of acceleration must be the foundation for an immediate massive effort to ensure that DOTS services are expanded quickly and effectively. The greater the delay, the greater the daily burden of entirely preventable illness and death.

Rapid gains in case detection under DOTS by all providers could potentially be made in the Americas, Europe, and Southeast Asia. Even so, a radically different approach will be required to lift global case detection rates from a likely plateau of 50 percent to the target of 70 percent. DOTS programs and public health authorities must work with nonparticipating providers to ensure they meet DOTS standards, especially in the private sector in Asia and from beyond the present limits of the public sector in Africa. These are the regions of the world that account for the vast majority of cases that are not yet detected by public health authorities. The urgent expansion of the DOTS strategy requires the coordinated efforts of all TB healthcare providers in a country, whether public, private, or voluntary.

Success in TB treatment is a prerequisite for DOTS expansion. Encouragingly, the global treatment success rate under DOTS was 82 percent in 2002 and should reach the target of 85 percent on time in 2005. But here again there are marked variations in rates between regions: from 71 percent in Africa to 93 percent in the Western Pacific. Fatal outcomes were most common in Africa, where a higher percentage of cases are HIV-positive, and Europe, where a higher percentage of cases are drug-resistant (eastern Europe) or occur among the elderly (western Europe).

Adapted strategies, especially for HIV-related tuberculosis and multidrug-resistant tuberculosis

In some countries, even full and successful DOTS expansion will not be sufficient on its own. New approaches have been developed to combat the threats of HIV-related TB and MDR-TB. Now the challenge is to scale up implementation.

HIV-related tuberculosis: two diseases, one patient

The greatest emergency in TB control arises from the HIV pandemic. The explosion of HIV-related TB has reversed decades of improvements in TB control, particularly in Sub-Saharan Africa and some states of the former Soviet Union. Now it threatens progress against TB in East and South Asian countries where the HIV epidemic is making new inroads

The surge in HIV infections has fueled the TB epidemic, just as TB is a leading killer of people with HIV. In several African countries, the number of TB cases has increased up to fourfold in the past decade, mainly as a result of the HIV epidemic. HIV infection multiplies the risk of developing active TB by more than 30-fold. Normally the progression from latent infection to clinical disease is a slow process, but for HIV co-infected patients it can be rapid and fatal. Because of their suppressed immune system, people with HIV and latent TB have a 5–15 percent annual risk of developing an active TB infection versus a 10 percent lifetime risk for those with latent TB alone. And HIV also increases the risk of recurrent TB after successful treatment.

Global figures mask extreme differences in national prevalence rates of HIV infection in new TB cases. Some countries (Afghanistan, Bangladesh, China, and Indonesia) have a rate under 1 percent. In others (South Africa and Zimbabwe), the rate is 60 percent or more. In all, it is estimated that some 11 million adults are co-infected with both TB and HIV—2 million in South Africa alone. An HIV epidemic can lead to dramatic increases in the number of people who contract TB, even in countries that have traditionally had a low TB incidence. In the United States, just over a quarter of TB cases are estimated to occur in HIV-positive individuals.

Twelve percent of all deaths from TB in 2000 were among HIV-positive people. Conversely, although TB is preventable and treatable, it is one of the

Without the correct drugs, MDR-TB is untreatable and in most cases fatal

most common causes of morbidity and death in HIV-positive adults living in developing countries.

This desperate and urgent situation poses some real challenges. Most of the recent successes in TB control have been in countries with low rates of HIV infection such as China, Peru, and Viet Nam. The task is much more difficult in settings where TB and HIV are both common.

Addressing both these deadly epidemics in a coordinated manner demands far-reaching changes in approaches and attitudes. Success will depend upon genuine and effective collaboration between the TB and HIV/AIDS treatment communities in implementing the adaptation of DOTS to HIV settings.

Multidrug-resistant tuberculosis

MDR-TB is also an increasing threat. WHO estimates that worldwide there are 300,000 new cases each year, and it has emerged in nearly every country of the world. TB patients in parts of Eastern Europe and Central Asia are 10 times more likely to have MDR-TB than people in the rest of the world. These populations are also facing the fastest growing HIV infection rates worldwide, compounding the challenges of TB control.

Seventy-nine percent of MDR-TB cases are now "super strains," resistant to at least three of the four main drugs used to cure TB. With no effective vaccine, everyone is vulnerable to infection simply by breathing in a droplet carrying a virulent drug-resistant strain.

TB can be transmitted from person to person but is fostered by poor provider prescribing, low-quality first-line drugs, or irregular drug supplies that interrupt patient medication. Or patients may themselves simply stop taking the drugs, because they feel better, for example, or because the six- to eight-month course of treatment is so long and stressful.

Without the correct drugs, MDR-TB is untreatable and in most cases fatal. Access to second-line drugs is essential, but they are not available to most sufferers. Even when it is available, the course of treatment takes much longer (18–24 months), its efficacy is lower, and adverse reaction rates are higher. Though curing "normal" TB is cheap and effective—a six-month course of medicines costs $10—treating drug-resistant TB can cost many times more. The Green Light Committee (GLC) has proven successful in preventing misuse of second-line drugs, promoting access to quality-assured drugs, and providing technical assistance to countries implementing DOTS-Plus. Its efforts must be urgently expanded.

Good TB control practices are associated with lower levels of resistance. In the worst affected areas, innovative "DOTS-Plus" schemes are being introduced. This involves diagnosing MDR-TB through quality-assured culture and drug susceptibility testing, and treating with second-line drugs under proper case management conditions. The pace of scaling up is quickening due to international endorsement of mainstreaming DOTS-Plus into DOTS, and to financial support from the Global Fund to Fight AIDS, Tuberculosis, and Malaria (GFATM).

TB strikes
poverty-
stricken
populations
hardest

Other adaptations to DOTS

DOTS is the most effective, large-scale strategy for the treatment of TB we have. But neither TB nor the challenges it presents remain static. There will be continuing need to evaluate and modify diagnostic and treatment protocols to address the changing features of the epidemic, as in the case of TB/HIV and MDR-TB. DOTS programs must also be flexible enough to meet the needs of patients with special requirements or living in particular conditions or geographical areas, especially those who are most vulnerable.

Priorities for action

Success in achieving the Millennium Development Goals target must mean halting the incidence of TB in every region and country of the world, not just in global terms. This demands a targeted strategy reflecting national characteristics. The Stop TB Partnership has already established a strategic focus on the 22 countries that together shoulder 80 percent of the global TB burden. Sub-Saharan Africa—which confronts a surge in HIV-related TB cases as well as endemic poverty—must also be a special focus of international support. At present, up to 70 percent of African people with HIV lack access to functioning DOTS programs.

TB strikes poverty-stricken populations hardest. Achieving the Millennium Development Goals targets for poverty will reduce susceptibility to TB, just as achieving the target for TB will help improve the economic and social condition of millions of TB sufferers and their families. Interventions to target the poor in particular, and to evaluate the equitable distribution of DOTS, should be a basic plank of approaches to TB control.

The UN Millennium Project Working Group on TB recommends the following priorities for action in order to achieve the target of halving TB prevalence and deaths by 2015:

1. Ensure access for all to high-quality TB care.
2. Address the TB/HIV emergency now.
3. Engage all primary care providers in high-quality TB care.
4. Partner with communities to stop TB.
5. Stop the spread of MDR-TB.
6. Accelerate the development of critically needed new tools.
7. Support the Global Plan to Stop TB.

1. Ensure access for all to high-quality tuberculosis care

All TB patients should have access to the universal standard of care that is based on proper diagnosis, treatment, and reporting consistent with the DOTS strategy. Hugely expanded access to quality treatment under DOTS is an immediate necessity.

While much has been achieved, and recent acceleration in access to DOTS quality care is encouraging, there is still a long way to go to achieve the targets.

Investment in TB interventions is a sound one, with immediate returns

Each year, there are 2 million unnecessary deaths from TB—a disease that is preventable and curable.

It is crucial to act now to increase the scope, quality, and impact of the key TB interventions. This requires concerted action on several fronts: national action, international coordination, and innovative support mechanisms. Advocacy and political support will have a vital role to play.

Investment in TB is a sound one, with immediate returns. Globally, TB costs more than $3.3 billion each year in lost productivity. For each $1 invested in DOTS, the expected return in increased economic output is more than $3.50 (for example, from increased productivity, deaths prevented, and hospital beds freed).

Technically, the massive drive required to ensure that every person with TB has access to the DOTS standard of care depends on consolidating and sustaining achievements so far, improving DOTS coverage and treatment success rates, and mainstreaming the adapted strategies to combat HIV-related TB and MDR-TB. Bringing these activities to successful outcomes will require a long-term commitment from national governments, donors, and the Stop TB Partnership in its broadest sense.

In many of the most affected countries, DOTS expansion is hampered by the extreme weakness of health services and infrastructure. The crisis in health service staffing—in terms of inadequate numbers, distribution, skills, and motivation—is particularly acute. Improving TB services, and achieving other Millennium Development Goals targets, will require strengthening health systems more generally. The issue of health systems is being addressed by a separate working group. TB programs alone cannot resolve all service delivery bottlenecks, but they must engage more actively with broad health sector issues and health system strengthening.

Implementing DOTS can contribute to better health systems. Examples include improved laboratory capacity, innovation in community care and public-private mix initiatives, improved documentation of health outcomes, and the potential for improved health management systems using the DOTS strategy as a model for a results-oriented health intervention.

Countries should plan to develop systems for routine reporting on TB cases and deaths, and on drug resistance. In the interim, population-based surveys of the prevalence of TB disease are recommended, especially in countries with high TB or HIV burdens.

2. Address the TB/HIV emergency now

To address the TB/HIV emergency, TB and HIV/AIDS partnerships must immediately step up collaboration to deliver the 2004 expanded strategy recommended by the WHO to control HIV-related TB (WHO 2004a, 2004c).

This strategy consists of interventions against TB and interventions against HIV (and therefore indirectly against TB). Its aims include:

Countries
and donors
must now
focus specific
attention on
combating
the TB/HIV
emergency

- Reducing TB incidence among people living with HIV/AIDS—through collaborative efforts to improve the performance of national TB programs, through provision of isoniazid preventative therapy for co-infected patients, and through earlier detection of active TB through intensified case finding. Interventions include full implementation of the DOTS strategy.
- Reducing HIV incidence and disease among TB patients—through providing voluntary counseling and testing for people at risk of HIV, and preventive methods and therapy. Interventions include, for example, providing condoms, treatment of sexually transmitted infections, safe injecting drug use, and antiretroviral treatment.
- Improving the care of people who are infected with both TB and HIV—through cross-training and collaborative care initiatives.

Taken together, these measures can prevent, treat, and cure TB among HIV-infected people, while reducing HIV infection, morbidity, and mortality among people with TB.

But an assessment carried out in October 2003 indicated that the key recommended interventions were so far being carried out only on a small scale. None of the 22 TB high-burden countries had implemented any collaborative activities on a national scale. Most neither routinely tested TB patients for HIV nor actively looked for TB among people infected with HIV. Few offered isoniazid preventive therapy, which WHO sees as an integral part of the package of care for those with both TB and HIV.

Countries and donors must now focus specific attention on combating the TB/HIV emergency. Tackling the immediate crisis requires an urgent and exceptional effort to maximize the benefit of current levels of funding and support from the international community. Work on the Stop TB Partnership's Global Plan II 2006–15 must identify the further levels of support needed to meet the Millennium Development target.

The task is essential but not simple. A catalogue of clinical, technical, and operational problems poses a major challenge to ensuring that every individual in need gets appropriate diagnosis and treatment. HIV infection massively increases the demands on TB programs, which are struggling to cope with the increased TB caseload. The rise in the number of people potentially ill with TB and needing to be tested is putting a strain on diagnostic services, which are hampered by lack of effective diagnostics. Extrapulmonary and smear-negative pulmonary TB cases, which are more difficult to diagnose, account for an increased proportion of total cases. There can be dangerous drug interactions between rifampicin, a cornerstone TB drug, and most antiretrovirals. Morbidity and mortality are higher, partly due to other, curable, HIV-related infections. The risk of TB recurrence is higher.

The expanded DOTS strategy to control HIV-related TB will be successful only through patient-centered, countrywide TB and HIV collaborative ser-

National TB programs should engage public, private, and voluntary TB care providers under their stewardship

vice delivery, complemented by a major initiative to strengthen health systems. There is growing financing for TB and HIV/AIDS programs but, within this, there needs to be strong support for fully financed joint efforts, not just parallel streams.

At the same time, greater priority must be given to the development of drugs, diagnostics, and vaccines that are reliable in HIV settings. New, faster acting drugs that are designed to be compatible with antiretroviral treatment are vital. More effective and user-friendly diagnostic tools are urgently needed. While the long-used method of smear microscopy continues to detect millions of patients, it is not detecting TB in a significant and growing proportion of patients in high-HIV settings. Where HIV is common, diagnosis must be accelerated so that TB is detected and treated earlier.

Operational research must be intensified to define the best strategies for joint management of the overlapping epidemics, including effective collaboration between TB and HIV programs at all levels.

3. Engage all primary care providers in high-quality tuberculosis care

Scaled-up TB control and action against HIV-related TB should be further integrated as a key component of primary care.

Decentralization, with ambulatory treatment at a facility as close as possible to the patient's home, provides patients with easier access to care. It could also ease pressure on hospitals, especially in settings struggling with high numbers of HIV patients.

TB control depends on effective diagnosis, treatment, and follow-up, mainly in primary care. Despite effective low-cost or free national TB programs, a significant number of TB patients opt for treatment by private practitioners. Faster progress in global TB control and care depends on ensuring all care providers deliver to all patients the DOTS international standard of care and support.

National TB programs should engage the full range of public, private, and voluntary TB care providers under their stewardship, with reform of regulatory provisions if necessary. This must cover government services, whether in the ministry of health (nationally and locally administered services) or not (for example, social security schemes, prisons, the military), and nongovernment services, such as NGOs, community groups, private practitioners, and employers.

This level of coordination in turn requires sustained political will and substantial funding and support from both national and international sources.

National TB programs should consider public-private mix approaches as a means to expand and strengthen DOTS, with an emphasis on improving case detection and treatment success.

The business sector—including state enterprises—has the potential to contribute to TB control, for example by including TB control measures in estab-

Scaling up the supply of effective TB services must go hand in hand with scaling up the demand for them

lished business sector health activities (especially in HIV/AIDS programs), and by supplying management and communications expertise.

4. Partner with communities to stop tuberculosis

Scaling up the supply of effective TB services must go hand in hand with scaling up the demand for them.

Government health providers have been the main focus of TB control activities. Success in the future demands a broader approach, including more active partnership with communities.

Through active recruitment and routine inclusion of community and grassroots organizations into the planning, implementation, and evaluation processes, national TB programs could be provided with essential local knowledge and experience. The programs must also become more responsive to the recommendations, needs, and concerns of such bodies.

These organizations can include civil society groups, employers, local NGOs, representatives of groups of TB patients, and HIV activists, as well as the local education sector and key multilateral organizations. HIV advocacy and care and support from within the communities affected by HIV/AIDS can play a vital role in supporting earlier case detection, broader access to DOTS, and higher completion rates. Informed, local participation is the most direct way to address obstructive misconceptions and to facilitate educational outreach.

Using neighbors and associates of people diagnosed with TB, MDR-TB, and HIV/AIDS to provide supervised services such as medication administration, routine care, and assistance has proven helpful in many low-income settings. In regions hit hardest by loss of health workers, expanding the pool of paid community health workers may be the only immediately available option to support the development and expansion of diagnostic outreach and treatment programs.

Appropriate communications and information strategies are vital. Brochures and posters are useful in literate communities where residents actively seek health information. But other tailored approaches are essential to engage the larger public. These include street rallies, speeches in places of worship, radio programs, television shows, and information at school and at work.

Donor and technical agencies should support countries in building capacity for advocacy, communications, and social mobilization at all levels, as a routine part of DOTS expansion plans. Information systems should reflect this effort by developing and reporting indicators that can monitor progress in these areas.

5. Stop the spread of multidrug-resistant tuberculosis

The emergence of MDR-TB needs to be tackled effectively and as swiftly as possible. There are three main areas of action.

Normal DOTS programs should be expanded, and fully and effectively implemented

First, normal DOTS programs should be expanded, and fully and effectively implemented, in order to minimize the conditions for further drug resistance to occur.

Second, treatment of MDR-TB requires that DOTS-Plus must be scaled up and mainstreamed into countrywide TB control plans. This is a matter of special urgency in areas where MDR-TB rates are already serious. DOTS-Plus is an adaptation of DOTS, providing a programmatic approach to the diagnosis and treatment of MDR-TB within the context of DOTS programs. Urgent support is needed for the Green Light Committee to allow them to provide technical assistance for programs wishing to implement and scale up DOTS-Plus.

Third, it is critical to develop new drugs to treat patients with MDR-TB. There needs to be a pipeline of novel drugs, administered in combinations to minimize the emergence of new resistances.

Investment is needed both to maintain financial support for existing second-line drugs and to develop new drugs.

Drug resistance information should be monitored as an indicator of the quality of treatment programs. At the moment, testing TB patients for drug resistance—like testing patients for HIV—tends to be handled as a separate exercise, but the goal should be to incorporate both into routine case surveillance.

6. Accelerate the development of critically needed new tools

Current diagnostics for TB are more than 100 years old, no vaccine has come to market since the 1920s, and most of the drugs used to treat the disease are more than 30 years old.

The chances of reaching the Millennium Development target for TB could be vastly improved through the development of new and better tools. Faster, simpler, more effective diagnostics are needed to speed case finding and allow more comprehensive identification of TB, especially in children and high-risk populations such as people with HIV. New drugs are needed to shorten and simplify treatment, to overcome resistant strains, and to allow treatment of latent infection. The greatest challenge—and potentially the greatest gain—lies in the development of a vaccine that is effective for people of all ages and in all settings.

In addition to academic and government research, three public-private partnerships dedicated to research and development have been created. They have yielded a pipeline of new TB drugs, the first TB vaccine trials in more than 80 years, and an array of innovative new projects in TB diagnostic technology. Donor agencies should increase their investments to sustain these early developments, and scale up portfolios of projects to secure the development and use of the best new tools that science can deliver.

The Stop TB Partnership should work to ensure that new tools respond to the greatest demands of users, and expedite testing and roll-out wherever TB is a major problem.

The GFATM is a critically important new funder of TB control

Greatly increased support is also needed for basic and applied science on TB and operational research on program effectiveness. Operational research is urgently needed to demonstrate the best approaches to scaling up services, strengthening TB/HIV collaboration, and serving those hardest to reach.

7. Support the Global Plan to Stop TB

The Global Plan to Stop TB 2001–05, and complementary national strategic plans, have provided the early roadmap for achieving the Millennium Development Goals targets and set the course for eventually eliminating TB as a public health problem. Long-term planning and sustainable financing are crucial to success. Work to extend the Global Plan to 2015 is already underway.

All those involved at global, national, and local levels should come together to invest in the Global Plan, implement its key interventions, and work together to secure its targets—halving TB prevalence and deaths by 2015.

The Stop TB Partnership is just beginning work on a comprehensive Global Plan to Stop TB II (2006–15). Updated figures for the resource requirements to achieve the Millennium Development Goals target for TB in line with the recommendations of this report will be provided as part of developing this Global Plan.

Previous estimates of an annual resource gap of at least $1 billion for global TB control and new tool development underestimate requirements for recommendations to expand DOTS, mainstream TB/HIV and DOTS-Plus interventions, and sustain the Global Drug Facility and Green Light Committee.

The updated estimates, when available, should be used to advocate for increased levels of funding for TB control and new tools for research and development that are commensurate with the global burden of TB and that will provide the full resources needed to reverse this epidemic.

The GFATM is a critically important new funder of TB control. Adequate GFATM funding and increased GFATM support for TB and TB/HIV efforts needs to be ensured. Increased technical support is needed for development and implementation of GFATM-financed projects, as well as programs supported by other sources of finance.

Conclusion

The target to halve the prevalence of TB disease and deaths by 2015 is certainly achievable. The basic pillars of a successful plan are understood and widely accepted. They include structures, strategies, and supplies.

What is needed now is expansion, adaptation, and investment of demonstrably successful approaches based on DOTS. On several fronts, the necessary instruments are already in place, though tackling TB/HIV effectively demands more far-reaching changes in approaches and attitudes. Also critical are the mainstreaming of DOTS-Plus into DOTS programs and intensified support to creating new drugs, diagnostics, and vaccines.

	Problem	Key interventions	Focus and level of interventions

Box 2
 	
Recommended key interventions to meet the Millennium Development Goals target for tuberculosis
	TB:
	
	2 million deaths and 9 million new cases per year.
		To ensure access for all to high quality TB care:
		• Implement the DOTS strategy:
		  1. Political commitment.
		  2. Diagnosis with sputum smear microscopy.
		  3. Standardized short-course chemotherapy.
		  4. Consistent supply of essential TB drugs.
		  5. Standardized recording and reporting systems.
		• Implement collaborative interventions against TB and against HIV, to control HIV-related TB.
		• Mainstream DOTS-Plus adaptation in high MDR-TB settings.
		• Accelerate development and use of new tools for diagnosis, treatment, and prevention.
			The full range of providers in the public and private sectors and the community should deliver the international standard of care, in line with the DOTS strategy.
			• Community partnership and outreach, grassroots mobilization.
			• Strategic focus on
			  1. 22 TB high-burden countries, which account for 80 percent of all TB cases.
			  2. Sub-Saharan Africa, because of poverty and HIV-related TB.
			  3. Poor people.
			• Public-private partnerships for developing new tools, and local engagement for testing new diagnostics, drugs, and vaccines.

The key interventions recommended in this report (box 2) must be accompanied by a broader initiative to strengthen depleted health systems. Success will require political commitment and effective advocacy and communications. Backed by sufficient and sustained support nationally and internationally over the next 10 years, these measures provide the blueprint for turning the tide of TB by 2015.

Chapter 1

The emergency of tuberculosis

Tuberculosis (TB) is a paradox of our modern age. In an era of unprecedented—if inequitably distributed—wealth and scientific advancement, nearly two million people die each year from an infectious disease for which proven, cost-effective treatments have been available for decades.

Thanks to the discovery of antibiotics and better living standards, the epidemics of "galloping consumption" that ravaged Europe and North America in the nineteenth and early twentieth centuries had become almost a thing of the past in industrialized countries almost half a century ago. But those gains have not been shared by the rest of the world.

More recently, there have been new threats. First, the emergence of HIV/AIDS has fueled the TB epidemic, just as TB has contributed to the HIV/AIDS epidemic. Because of their suppressed immune systems, people co-infected with HIV and TB are many times more likely to develop active TB. In several African countries, the number of TB cases has increased up to fourfold in the past decade, mainly as a result of the HIV epidemic.

Second, the world has learned the hard way about the resilience of the TB bacillus. Arising from human misuse of anti-TB drugs, mutating forms of the bacterium have developed resistance to the standard forms of treatment. Thousands of people are becoming infected with resistant strains of TB that are more difficult, more complex, and more expensive to treat.

In 1993, the World Health Organization (WHO) declared TB to be a global health emergency. Despite considerable progress since then in developing institutional and strategic approaches, TB not only remains an emergency but its threat continues to grow.

One-third of the world's population is latently infected with the bacillus that causes TB (*Mycobacterium tuberculosis*). Although only a small proportion of these people will develop active TB, the sheer scale is startling. In 2002,

Control of TB rests on interruption of its transmission

there were nearly 9 million new cases of TB (WHO 2004j). Of these, nearly 4 million people had sputum smear–positive pulmonary TB—that is, the form of TB affecting the lungs that is most infectious. Normally the progression to clinical disease is a slow process, but for HIV co-infected patients, it can be rapid and fatal. Today TB is still one of the world's leading causes of death and of the global burden of disease. It is a major killer of women, rivaling maternal mortality.

TB afflicts the poor above all. Vulnerability to active TB has always been strongly correlated with the conditions and consequences of poverty, such as malnutrition, inadequate and overcrowded housing, and unsanitary working conditions. Ninety-five percent of all TB sufferers live in developing countries. Most are poor people ages 15–54, who should be in their prime productive and reproductive years (WHO 2002). The impact of millions of individual deaths is multiplied by the wider impact on families and communities devastated by the loss of social and economic support networks. Too often TB traps patients and their families in a cycle of disease and impoverishment, and it disrupts the social fabric of society through the stigmatization of the sufferers (WHO/Stop TB 2001). TB exacts an appallingly high cost for patients and their families, for their health services, and for their societies as a whole. Urgent and effective action is needed now.

The DOTS strategy to control tuberculosis

Control of TB rests on interruption of its transmission through the rapid identification and cure of infectious cases.

Fortunately, there is an internationally recommended strategy for delivering the basics of TB case finding and cure, known as DOTS (originally derived from directly observed therapy, short-course) (box 1.1). DOTS is not simply a clinical approach to patients, but rather a management strategy for public health systems that includes political commitment and technical elements (WHO 2004j). The principles of the DOTS strategy apply to all TB patients, of all ages and with all forms of TB (box 1.2).

Box 1.1

The five elements of the DOTS strategy for tuberculosis control

Source: WHO 2004n.

1. Political commitment to sustained TB control activities
2. Case detection by sputum-smear microscopy among symptomatic patients self-reporting to health services
3. A standardized treatment regimen of six to eight months for at least all sputum smear–positive cases, with directly observed therapy for at least the initial two months
4. A regular, uninterrupted supply of all essential anti-TB drugs
5. A standardized recording and reporting system that allows assessment of treatment results for each patient and of the TB control program performance overall

Box 1.2

DOTS and the patient

Source: WHO 2004n.

- Patients with infectious TB are identified using microscopy (bacilli visible in a sputum smear).
- Health and community workers and trained volunteers observe and record patients swallowing the full course of the correct dosage of anti-TB medicines, over six to eight months.
- Sputum smear testing is repeated after two months to check progress, and again at the end of treatment.
- A recording and reporting system documents patients' progress and the final outcome of treatment.

The basic principles of the DOTS strategy were not new when it was introduced in the early 1990s. TB control professionals had generally agreed that the best approach included case finding among patients presenting mainly with chronic cough to general health services, short-course chemotherapy, ensuring patient compliance with treatment, maintaining adequate drug supply, and sound reporting and recording systems. The crucial innovations were the public health packaging and promotion of the strategy, and the addition of the human element—having healthcare workers or trained volunteers form a close bond with their patients to help them successfully complete the arduous six- to eight-month treatment, involving taking up to one hundred doses of medication.

"Stop TB—Use DOTS" became a clarion call for TB control programs around the world. The World Bank's *World Development Report 1993: Health* (1993) concluded that TB control using DOTS was one of the most cost-effective of all health interventions. This finding has been reinforced by more recent studies on cost-effectiveness. Globally, TB costs more than $3.3 billion each year in lost productivity. Investment in TB control and treatment is a sound one, with immediate returns (see, for example, de Jonghe and others 1994; Jha 1998; World Bank 1993). For each dollar invested in DOTS, the expected return in increased economic output is more than $3.50 (for example, from increased productivity, deaths prevented, and hospital beds freed).

Despite widespread agreement on the need to implement DOTS worldwide, more than 10 years later residents of some of the world's poorest communities where TB incidence is highest have yet to see the benefits of the proven DOTS remedy. Intensified implementation and expansion of DOTS control strategies are needed as a minimum if TB trends are to be deflected from their present trajectory (Stop TB Partnership/WHO 2001).

The need for modern tools: diagnostics, drugs, and vaccines

One prime and urgent need to complement DOTS is for a modern armamentarium to beat back TB and combat the challenges posed by HIV/AIDS and multidrug-resistant TB (MDR-TB). It is critical to update TB control with modern tools designed for ease of use in poor countries:

It is critical to update TB control with modern tools designed for use in poor countries

- New diagnostics to replace the basic sputum smear microscopy test, which was developed over 120 years ago, with cheap, quick, reliable tests that are effective in screening for latent TB and in diagnosing TB and MDR-TB.
- New drugs to shorten and simplify the treatment of TB and to treat MDR-TB and latent TB infection more effectively.
- A new vaccine to replace the current Bacillus Camille Guerin vaccine, first used in 1921, which provides moderate protection against severe childhood forms of TB but has little effect on the development of the predominant pulmonary form of the disease in adults.

The good news is that, in addition to existing research bodies, three new research agencies have been formed to ensure the delivery of better and affordable diagnostics, drugs, and—ultimately—vaccines: the Foundation for Innovative New Diagnostics, the Global Alliance for TB Drug Development, and the Aeras Global TB Vaccine Foundation. Each has adopted a public-private partnership approach and aims to create and to manage a portfolio within its field. The resulting products will leverage earlier investments in TB control to give TB patients and healthcare workers the best tools that modern science can deliver.

The Millennium Development Goals

At the United Nations Millennium Summit in September 2000, world leaders placed development at the heart of the global political agenda by adopting the Millennium Declaration. All 191 UN member states have pledged to meet the eight Millennium Development Goals.[1] Together, the Millennium Development Goals constitute an ambitious agenda to improve the human condition significantly by 2015. There are clear goals, each with its own targets and indicators, for reducing poverty, hunger, disease, illiteracy, environmental degradation, and discrimination against women (see Goals on page xviii).

TB is covered by the target to have halted and begun to reverse the incidence of HIV/AIDS, malaria, and other major diseases by 2015 (box 1.3). The TB-specific indicators relate to both impact measures (prevalence and death rates) and process measures (cases detected and cured under the DOTS strategy).

Given the huge burden of disease and mortality created by TB, the Working Group on TB feels strongly that TB should be explicitly named in Millennium Goal 6. It should be noted that the United Nations has set TB-specific indicators under Target 8. The working group therefore recommends that:

- Millennium Development Goal 6 should be amended to read "Combat HIV/AIDS, malaria, TB, and other diseases."
- The global TB control target should be to halve the prevalence of TB disease and deaths between 1990 and 2015, a measurable target that is demanding yet feasible.

Millennium Development Goal 6: Combat HIV/AIDS, malaria, and other diseases.

Target 8: Have halted by 2015 and begun to reverse the incidence of malaria and other major diseases.

Indicator 23: Prevalence and death rates associated with tuberculosis.

Indicator 24: Proportion of tuberculosis cases detected and cured under DOTS (internationally recommended tuberculosis control strategy).

Recommended tuberculosis control target: to halve the prevalence of tuberculosis disease and deaths between 1990 and 2015.

The objectives set by the Millennium Development Goal require a commitment to controlling TB worldwide. The Millennium Declaration goes further, insisting that the means for achieving that end must reflect specified fundamental values, including solidarity: "Global challenges must be managed in a way that distributes the costs and burdens fairly in accordance with basic principles of equity and social justice."[2]

The full set of Millennium Development Goals provides a crucial framework for helping reverse the TB epidemic by linking TB control to overall health sector development and development activities in general. Action taken to meet the TB target will both reflect and contribute to action taken to meet other targets, particularly those relating to poverty, gender issues, HIV/AIDS, and access to essential medicines.

Indicator 24 for TB echoes earlier targets set by the World Health Assembly in 1991, which were to detect 70 percent of new infectious cases and to treat successfully 85 percent of detected sputum-positive patients.

Originally intended for achievement by the year 2000, reaching the World Health Assembly targets was postponed to 2005 when it became clear that most of the countries with the highest burden of disease would not meet the 2000 deadline (box 1.4). The target of an 85 percent treatment success rate should be attained globally on time in 2005. However, it will also be necessary to address the marked regional differences, given substantially poorer treatment success rates in Africa (71 percent) and in Eastern Europe (70 percent). Timely success in reaching the case detection target is proving more elusive although, encouragingly, progress appears to have been accelerating since 2000.

Evidence suggests that meeting these World Health Assembly process targets could reduce TB incidence by 6 percent per year, effectively halving TB

• Detect at least 70 percent of new infectious cases of TB.

• Successfully treat at least 85 percent of those detected.

**Meeting
these process
targets could
reduce TB
incidence
by 6 percent
per year**

incidence within 10 years (MSF 2004). These process targets are critical bench-marks. Achieving them should lead to reaching the Millennium Development Goal's impact target of reversing the incidence of TB everywhere except in high HIV areas.

The UN Millennium Project Working Group on TB and the Stop TB Partnership

As a core part of its work, the UN Millennium Project is working with UN country teams and governments in selected low-income countries to identify the best ways to integrate Millennium Development Goals (MDG) targets and time horizons into existing policy processes. This includes helping each government in a three-step planning process:

- Conducting a detailed MDG needs assessment that estimates the long-term infrastructural, human, and financial resources needed to achieve the Goals.
- Mapping out a strategy through 2015 that outlines the policies, institutions, and investments needed to achieve the Millennium Development Goals, building on the MDG needs assessment.
- Constructing the short-term (3–5 year) poverty reduction strategy and budgetary framework necessary to initiate the long-term MDG strategy.

The Working Group on TB drew from existing material to develop four country case studies to begin discussing how the countries concerned can best meet the MDG target of reversing the incidence of TB by 2015. A detailed study has been undertaken for Kenya, and a briefer analysis is provided for three other countries: Cambodia, the Dominican Republic, and Ethiopia.

The Working Group on TB has worked closely with the Stop TB Partnership, an international coalition of governments, organizations, and individuals committed to controlling, and eventually eliminating, TB as a public health problem in the world. It has over 300 partners meeting regularly at a Partners' Forum, a Secretariat hosted by the WHO, a Global Drug Facility (GDF), and seven working groups to address key priorities: DOTS expansion; TB/HIV; DOTS-Plus for treating MDR-TB; new drug, diagnostics, and vaccine development; and advocacy and communications.

The Stop TB Partnership has committed itself to a range of short-, medium-, and long-term global targets:

- The World Health Assembly targets for 2005 described above.
- An ambitious target for 2010 of reducing the global burden of TB disease (deaths and prevalence) by 50 percent, compared with 2000 levels (derived from the G8 Okinawa 2010 targets).
- The MDG target to have halted and begun to reverse the incidence of TB by 2015.
- A longer term target that the global incidence of TB disease should be less than 1 per million population by 2050.

The global TB control target should be to halve the prevalence of disease and death by 2015

While the Working Group on TB is an independent entity with its own specific outputs and recommendations, the two groups are closely aligned and share a common view of the key strategies needed to defeat TB.

In particular, the working group has drawn from the *Global Plan to Stop TB 2001–2005* launched by the then newly established Global Partnership in 2001, and its subsequent progress report published in 2004 (Stop TB/WHO 2001; 2004). The full range of strategies identified by the *Global Plan to Stop TB* constitutes a comprehensive approach for both implementation and research that will be essential in meeting the Millennium Development Goals target of reversing the incidence of TB by 2015. The Stop TB Partnership in turn has formally agreed that its next Global Plan should cover the period 2006–15, to align with the MDG target for TB.

The Working Group on TB is also indebted to the work of a committee—the 2nd Ad Hoc Committee on the TB Epidemic—established in 2003 by the Global Partnership's DOTS Expansion Working Group to review progress in TB control and constraints, based on a series of consultations. The committee's recommendations and its background document are cited extensively throughout this report (Stop TB Partnership/WHO 2004b).[3]

Recommendations
- Millennium Development Goal 6 should be amended to read: "Combat HIV/AIDS, malaria, tuberculosis, and other diseases" instead of "Combat HIV/AIDS, malaria, and other diseases."
- To provide a measurable target that is demanding but feasible, in practice the global TB control target should be to halve the prevalence of TB disease and deaths by 2015.

The global tuberculosis epidemic and tuberculosis control

This section of the report summarizes key data and findings on the current status of the global TB epidemic and of TB control, and then analyzes the implications for achieving the Millennium Development Goals indicators for TB.

Global achievements

The realization in the late 1990s that the World Health Assembly targets for TB would not be achieved for the millennium stimulated a fresh and vigorous commitment to international cooperation and action. As a result, the last few years have seen some major achievements, particularly in organizational and strategic terms. A 1998 Ad Hoc Committee on the TB Epidemic painted a compelling picture of the main constraints to effective TB control. Since then:

- Most important of all, countries have made real progress in providing more people with access to good-quality TB treatment under DOTS. Currently, 180 countries out of 210 are implementing DOTS, and the percentage of their populations covered by DOTS programs has increased steadily.
- The milestone Conference on TB and Sustainable Development in Amsterdam in 2000 brought together ministers from 20 of the 22 TB high-burden countries with high-level representatives of UN agencies, technical agencies, and donor countries. The Amsterdam Declaration formalized renewed political commitment to time-bound targets to stop TB.
- The Stop TB Partnership and its working groups have been established. The Partnership has harnessed widespread support to ensure that every TB patient has access to treatment and cure, to stop transmission of TB, to protect vulnerable populations from infection, and to reduce the social and economic toll that this disease exerts on families, communities, and nations.

The global community continues to face an enormous challenge

- The Stop TB Partnership has developed a Global Plan to Stop TB 2001–2005, setting out plans for the actions and investment needed to achieve the 2005 World Health Association targets—a plan that is now to be extended to 2015 to ensure that the Millennium Development Target for TB is met. Also in 2001, the World Health Organization (WHO) published the Global DOTS Expansion Plan.
- The establishment of a Global Drug Facility and a Green Light Committee has improved the availability, affordability, and quality of first- and second-line drugs respectively.
- Funding flows for TB control have increased, including through the Global Fund to Fight AIDS, Tuberculosis, and Malaria (GFATM). After its first four rounds of applications, the GFATM projects an additional 3.5 million TB cases will be treated under DOTS over five years.
- An unambiguous commitment to new tools and, in addition to ongoing academic and government research, the creation of novel public-private partnerships for new drugs, diagnostics, and vaccines has reinvigorated a stalled environment for research and development. The Global TB Alliance, the Foundation for Innovative New Diagnostics (FIND), and Aeras all use public and private approaches dedicated to developing affordable and better tools for use in high-burden environments.

Despite all these efforts, the global community continues to face an enormous challenge in reducing the global burden of TB.

Overview of the tuberculosis epidemic

Incidence rates vary dramatically around the world (map 2.1 and table 2.1). Heavily industrialized countries in North America and Western Europe have markedly lower rates than the developing countries of Sub-Saharan Africa, parts of Asia, and countries within Eastern Europe. Of the 15 countries with the highest estimated incidence rates per capita, 13 (excluding only Timor-Leste and Cambodia) are in Africa, and in most, the prevalence of HIV infection among TB patients is high.[1]

Poverty, HIV, and multidrug-resistant tuberculosis (MDR-TB) are key factors driving the epidemic. The rate for cases reported to WHO for all forms of TB has been rising quickly in African countries with high HIV prevalence (in eastern and southern African countries, this rate rose by 7 percent per year, 1997–2002), and in Eastern Europe, mainly the former Soviet Union (where the rate rose by 5 percent per year)—though the rate of increase has been slowing in both sets of countries since the mid-1990s. In most other regions of the world, the case notification rate has been roughly stable or in decline.

Tuberculosis high-burden countries

In order to achieve its own targets, the Stop TB Partnership is focusing its efforts on 22 high-burden countries. These are the countries with the highest

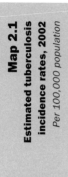

Map 2.1

Estimated tuberculosis
incidence rates, 2002

Per 100,000 population

Source: WHO 2004j.

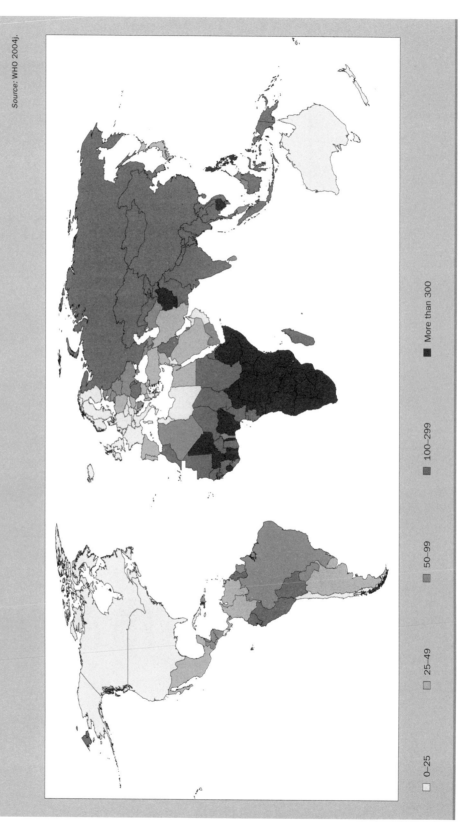

0–25   25–49   50–99   100–299   More than 300

Table 2.1
Estimated incidence of tuberculosis, by region, 2002

Source: WHO 2004.

Region	Population (thousands)	All cases		Smear-positive cases		
		Number (thousands)	Rate per 100,000 population	Number (thousands)	Rate per 100,000 population	Regional proportion of global total (percent)
Developed regions	992,756	184	19	83	8	2
Countries in Commonwealth of Independent States (CIS)	280,970	324	115	145	52	4
European countries in CIS	207,193	244	118	109	52	3
Asian countries in CIS	73,776	81	109	36	49	1
Developing regions	4,948,703	8,289	168	3,660	74	94
Africa	831,041	2,528	304	1,077	130	29
Northern Africa	147,018	74	51	33	23	1
Sub-Saharan Africa	684,023	2,454	359	1,044	153	28
Latin America and Caribbean	534,526	354	66	158	30	4
Asia	3,574,697	5,391	151	2,418	68	61
Eastern Asia	1,374,838	1,550	113	697	51	18
South Asia	1,480,287	2,507	169	1,122	76	28
Southeastern Asia	535,611	1,231	230	552	103	14
Western Asia	183,961	103	56	46	25	1
Oceania	8,440	16	189	7	84	0
World	6,222,429	8,798	141	3,888	62	100

In 2002 the number of countries implementing the DOTS strategy increased to 180

estimated absolute number of new TB cases. Together they account for some 80 percent of all new TB cases. India alone accounts for 20 percent, and China for a further 17 percent (table 2.2).

Prevalence and death rates associated with tuberculosis (Millennium Development Goals indicator 23)

Table 2.3 indicates the progress being made toward meeting the Millennium Development Goals and World Health Assembly targets. It gives WHO's best estimates of regional rates for TB prevalence (sputum smear–positive disease) and mortality from all forms of TB for 2000 (until recently, understood by WHO to be the baseline year for the Millennium Development Goals indicators), and 2002 (the latest year for which data are available). The Millennium Development Goals baseline year has now been confirmed as 1990. The 1990 TB baseline figures are being computed but were not available in time for this report.

Table 2.3 shows two sets of figures for TB prevalence and mortality: the first excludes people infected with HIV, in line with routine Millennium Development Goal reports, to avoid double-counting with HIV figures for prevalence and deaths. The second set includes people infected with HIV, to show the full impact of TB. The table also compares estimates by region of DOTS detection rates in 2000 and 2002, and treatment success rates for 2000 and 2001.

Overview of global tuberculosis control

Millennium Development Goals indicator 24 is the proportion of TB cases detected and cured under DOTS.[2] This summary of the current status of global TB control covers implementation of the DOTS strategy: the number of countries implementing the strategy, cases detected, treatment success, and progress toward the World Health Assembly targets for 2005.

Number of countries implementing the DOTS strategy

In 2002, the number of countries implementing the DOTS strategy increased to 180 out of 210—an increase of 25 over 2001. By the end of 2002, 69 percent of the world's population lived in administrative areas of countries where the DOTS strategy was theoretically available. In practice, however, a range of geographic, financial, and social barriers means that not all TB patients within these areas actually had access to DOTS (Elzinga, Raviglione, and Maher 2004).

Proportion of tuberculosis cases detected under DOTS (Indicator 24)

Case detection and treatment success rates are critical markers of progress. The 1.4 million smear-positive cases notified by DOTS programs in 2002 represent 37 percent of the estimated incidence (see table 2.3). This is just over half way to the World Health Assembly target of 70 percent case detection by 2005. This is a large gap to be bridged though, encouragingly, case detection rates under DOTS programs appear to have accelerated since 2000.

Table 2.2
Estimated incidence of tuberculosis in the 22 high-burden countries, 2002

Source: WHO 2004j.

	Country	Population (thousands)	All cases		Smear-positive cases		Cumulative incidence (percent)
			Number (thousands)	Rate per 100,000 population	Number (thousands)	Rate per 100,000 population	
1	India	1,049,549	1,761	168	787	75	20
2	China	1,294,867	1,459	113	656	51	37
3	Indonesia	217,131	557	256	250	115	43
4	Nigeria	120,911	368	304	159	132	47
5	Bangladesh	143,809	318	221	143	99	51
6	Pakistan	149,911	272	181	122	81	54
7	Ethiopia	68,961	255	370	110	159	57
8	Philippines	78,580	251	320	113	144	60
9	South Africa	44,759	250	558	102	227	62
10	Congo, Dem. Rep.	51,201	196	383	85	167	65
11	Russian Federation	144,082	182	126	81	56	67
12	Kenya	31,540	170	540	70	223	69
13	Viet Nam	80,278	155	192	69	86	70
14	Tanzania	36,276	132	363	56	155	72
15	Brazil	176,257	110	62	49	28	73
16	Uganda	25,004	94	377	41	164	74
17	Zimbabwe	12,835	88	683	35	271	75
18	Mozambique	18,537	81	436	34	182	76
19	Thailand	62,193	80	128	35	57	77
20	Afghanistan	22,930	76	333	34	150	78
21	Cambodia	13,810	76	549	33	242	79
22	Myanmar	48,852	75	154	33	68	80
	High-burden countries	3,892,274	7,005	180	3,100	80	80

Table 2.3
Tuberculosis prevalence, mortality, and DOTS detection rates by region, 2000 and 2002, and treatment success rates by region, 2000 and 2001

Region	Prevalence per 100,000 population (excluding HIV positive)		Prevalence per 100,000 population (including HIV positive)		Mortality per 100,000 population per year (excluding HIV positive)		Mortality per 100,000 population per year (including HIV positive)		DOTS detection rates[a] (percent)		Treatment success[b] (percent)	
	2000	2002	2000	2002	2000	2002	2000	2002	2000	2002	2000	2001
Developed regions	24	21	24	21	2	2	2	2	22	39	78	73
Countries in Commonwealth of Independent States (CIS)	150	161	151	163	16	18	17	19	12	16	76	75
European countries in CIS	156	170	158	173	17	19	18	20	4	5	68	67
Asian countries in CIS	133	135	133	135	14	15	14	15	37	47	78	77
Developing regions	332	306	338	313	32	30	37	35	28	37	82	82
Africa	388	414	420	450	43	46	69	72	38	44	73	72
Northern Africa	55	52	55	52	4	4	4	4	82	81	88	85
Sub-Saharan Africa	460	491	500	536	52	55	83	86	36	43	72	71
Latin America / Caribbean	99	91	100	92	10	9	10	10	43	45	81	83
Asia	354	313	355	314	33	30	34	31	24	34	88	88
Eastern Asia	268	265	268	266	21	20	21	21	28	28	94	96
South Asia	413	343	415	345	42	36	43	38	14	30	83	85
Southeastern Asia	505	432	507	434	48	43	50	44	39	50	86	86
Western Asia	85	84	85	84	9	9	9	9	26	25	81	83
Oceania	455	388	457	390	41	39	42	40	13	20	76	76
World	274	254	279	260	26	25	31	29	28	37	82	82

a. DOTS detection rate is the proportion of estimated new smear-positive cases notified to WHO by DOTS programs.

b. Treatment success is proportion of new smear-positive cases treated successfully under DOTS.

Source: WHO 2004j.

A WHO report
suggests
that getting
above the
50 percent
detection
rate will be
challenging

Some further gains in case detection could be made rapidly in three regions of the world by ensuring that the diagnosis and treatment of known TB patients meet DOTS standards. This could enable the target for case-finding to be met (or nearly approached) in the Americas and Europe, and significant gains could be made in Southeast Asia. In other regions, there is little scope for similar approaches. The overall effect would be to raise the figure for global case detection under DOTS from 37 percent to 50 percent—an improvement, but a figure still substantially below the 70 percent target.

The 2004 WHO report suggests that getting above the 50 percent detection rate will be challenging. It describes two main obstacles (WHO 2004j). First, to reach the 70 percent target by 2005—or indeed at all—DOTS programs must recruit cases that would not otherwise have been notified in the public sector. Even in countries with full geographic DOTS coverage, patients may remain unregistered because they receive care from health providers not linked to the national TB programs (for example, from private practitioners, academic institutions, NGOs, and traditional healers). Indeed, even some government health facilities may not be linked to the national TB program or follow its standards (for example, social security schemes, prisons, and army health facilities) (WHO 2004j).

Second, the smear-positive detection rate within DOTS areas has remained roughly constant since 1996 (the average is 49 percent). This suggests that almost all the gains in case detection have been made by geographical expansion of DOTS programs, and not by increasing case finding within DOTS areas. If so, the case detection rate would still be roughly 50 percent even if the whole world had access to DOTS.

Some high-burden countries do show signs of a slow improvement in case finding within DOTS areas, but these are much slower than the improvements made by extending DOTS to new areas. Six countries—India, South Africa, Indonesia, Pakistan, Bangladesh, and the Philippines—together accounted for over 60 percent of the additional smear-positive cases detected under DOTS in 2002. These were primarily responsible for the acceleration in case finding. India alone accounted for 28 percent of the additional cases, while having 20 percent of the world's caseload of TB.

Proportion of tuberculosis cases cured under DOTS (Indicator 24)
The cure rate among the 1.2 million new sputum smear–positive cases registered for treatment in DOTS programs in 2001 was 73 percent. A further 9.2 percent completed treatment without laboratory confirmation of cure. This means that the reported overall treatment success rate under DOTS was 82 percent, against the target for 2005 of 85 percent. Comparison of treatment results for eight consecutive cohorts (1994–2001) shows that the overall success rates have been above 80 percent under DOTS since 1998.

**The outcomes
of treatment
were far
worse in non-
DOTS areas**

However, in an assessment across the various WHO regions, treatment success rates under DOTS varied from 71 percent in Africa to 93 percent in the Western Pacific. Fatal outcomes were most common:

- In Africa (7 percent), where a higher fraction of cases are HIV positive.
- In Europe (6 percent), where a higher fraction of cases are drug resistant (eastern Europe) or occur among the elderly (western Europe).

National TB programs in Africa could do substantially better by reducing the proportion of patients lost from DOTS cohorts, which amounted to 21 percent of patients in 2001. Treatment interruption (default) was most frequent in the African (10 percent), Eastern Mediterranean (7 percent), and Southeast Asian (7 percent) regions. Transfer without follow-up was also especially high in Africa (7 percent). Although the ultimate target is for countrywide coverage with DOTS, TB control programs are advised not to expand case detection until high treatment success rates have been secured. A proportion of patients will remain chronically infectious and continue to spread TB if they are given less than a fully curative course of treatment.

In DOTS areas, over 186,000 cases were registered for re-treatment in 2001, with an overall success rate of 73 percent. More failures and deaths are expected in any case among patients being treated on a second or subsequent occasion, but the main reason for the low success rate for 2000 and 2001 cohorts is the high default rate. Good follow-up is vital to increasing the number of people cured of TB.

The quality of reporting and the outcomes of treatment were far worse in non-DOTS areas, with only 5 of 22 high-burden countries reporting results from non-DOTS areas and some data discrepancies. The overall treatment success rate was very low because outcomes were not evaluated for the majority of patients in India. Among cases registered for treatment, only 25 percent were cured and 40 percent were successfully treated. The death rate among evaluated patients was lower than in DOTS programs, but there will have been further deaths among the much higher proportion of patients lost to follow-up.

Progress toward the World Health Assembly targets for 2005

The World Health Assembly targets for 2005 of 70 percent case detection and 85 percent treatment success rates are the process interim indicators for the Millennium Development Goals target. By 2002, 18 countries (out of 173 countries providing the necessary data) appear to have reached, or be close to reaching, both targets. However, together these countries accounted for only 15 percent of all new smear-positive cases of TB in 2001.

Viet Nam was still the only current high-burden country to have reached both targets. Peru did so at an earlier stage and is no longer a high-burden country. Three high-burden countries—Brazil, Russia, and Uganda—had low rates both for case detection (less than 50 percent) and treatment success (less than 70 percent).

Real progress is being made. But it is too slow

Real progress is being made. Of 145 countries that provided data for both 2000 and 2001 cohorts:

- Just over a quarter (27 percent or 39 countries) improved case detection by more than 5 percent.
- Nearly a half (46 percent or 66 countries) showed higher treatment success rates for the 2001 cohort.

But progress is too slow. Based on current trends, WHO expects the global smear-positive detection rate to be about 50 percent by 2005, falling very substantially short of the target of 70 percent (WHO 2004j). The global target of an 85 percent treatment success rate should be attained by 2005, albeit with some significant regional variations (WHO 2004o).

To accelerate progress toward achieving the global targets and to sustain achievement of those targets in order to reach the Millennium Development Goals target for TB, WHO's Executive Board is to recommend to the next World Health Assembly in 2005 that (among other measures) there should be intensified support to member states in developing capacity and improving the performance of national TB control programs—within the broad context of strengthening health systems—and in improving collaboration between TB and HIV programs.

Among the 22 TB high-burden countries, the six most commonly identified constraints to planning and implementing DOTS in 2003 (WHO 2004j) are:

- Lack of qualified staff—major deficiencies in staff at the central level, and in the qualifications of staff at the peripheral level, are seen as the greatest barrier to reaching the targets for case detection and cure.
- Poor monitoring and evaluation—timely and reliable data are essential for planning corrective action and monitoring trends.
- Inadequate infrastructure—lack of roads and vehicles, poor communications networks, unreliable or nonexistent electricity supplies, inadequate buildings and equipment, and weak primary healthcare systems are major constraints.
- Weak laboratories—such as poor laboratory quality control, the lack of a laboratory network, or limited access to laboratory services.
- Poor involvement in DOTS of private or non-national TB program public providers—despite some limited public-private mix projects (such as those in India and the Philippines), inadequate partnership in DOTS across all TB service providers is a major obstacle.
- Limited commitment to, and capacity for, implementing DOTS in peripheral health services—following decentralization, several high-burden countries are constrained by their lack of capacity at the periphery to handle what were previously central responsibilities. In some cases, there are problems about local political support and ensuring the proper distribution of funding for TB control programs.

The greatest emerging threat to TB control arises from the HIV pandemic

In addition, several further constraints hampered TB control efforts in some high-burden countries:

- Weak and unstable political commitment.
- Increasing HIV-related TB.
- Limited access to DOTS by some of the population.
- Low public awareness of TB and its treatment, plus stigma about having TB.
- Administrative constraints, or policies inconsistent with DOTS.
- Unreliable drug supply or underdeveloped drug policy.
- Insufficient funds.

DOTS is remarkably effective. Recent experience in China suggests that implementation of DOTS with high cure rates led to a fall in the prevalence of TB by about 30 percent after seven years. The proportion of smear-positive patients who had previously been treated fell from 50 percent to 13 percent after seven years. If DOTS is equally successful in its governmental roll-out to the rest of China, the prevalence rate could be cut by 50 percent before 2015.

The case study on scaling up DOTS in China (box 2.1) also highlights characteristic challenges ahead: the need for strong political commitment and appropriate funding in all provinces, shortfalls in the number and quality of staff, inadequate infrastructure in poor areas, understrength monitoring and evaluation, and weaknesses in institutional communications.

If the Millennium Development Goals target is to be achieved, the deficiencies facing countries will need to be addressed.

Tuberculosis and HIV

The greatest emerging threat to TB control arises from the HIV pandemic. It has reversed decades of improvements in TB control, particularly in Sub-Saharan Africa and some states of the former Soviet Union. Now HIV-related TB threatens progress against TB in East and South Asian countries where the HIV epidemic is making new inroads.

HIV is deeply deleterious on several crucial counts. HIV-positive people are probably more susceptible to infection with *M. tuberculosis* in the first place. HIV is certainly the most powerful known risk factor for reactivation of latent TB infection. People with latent TB alone have a 10–20 percent risk of developing active TB in the course of their lives. For people with latent TB and HIV, however, the annual risk is 5–15 percent. This risk increases with increasing immunosuppression.

HIV increases not only the risk but also the rate of progression of recent or latent *M. tuberculosis* infection to disease. HIV also increases the risk of recurrent TB after successful TB treatment.

It is little surprise therefore that countries with a generalized HIV epidemic—most notably those in Sub-Saharan Africa—have faced a rapidly deteriorating TB crisis.

Box 2.1

**Scaling up
DOTS in China**

Source: WHO 2004j.

Despite formidable challenges, the two most populous countries in the world, China and India, are moving to scale up DOTS quickly.

With a population of 1.3 billion, China has 1.4 million new cases of TB each year, second only to India. In 1991, a DOTS TB control project was introduced in half the country with assistance from the World Bank. Free TB diagnosis and treatment have been provided through a network of dispensaries, while in non-DOTS areas, most patients have to pay. This project has successfully diagnosed, treated, and cured more cases of TB than any other DOTS program to date.

Comparison of national surveys undertaken in 1990 and 2000 suggest that, in the DOTS project areas, the prevalence of TB fell by about 30 percent after seven years, compared with an insignificant change in non-project areas (Dye and Watt 2004). The number of recurrent cases has fallen dramatically in DOTS areas almost certainly because of improved cure rates. Of smear-positive patients presenting at dispensaries, the proportion who had previously been treated fell from 50 percent to 13 percent after seven years.

The government of China plans to expand DOTS coverage to 100 percent of the country by 2005. If DOTS is equally successful in the rest of China, the prevalence rate could be cut by 50 percent before 2015.

However, despite the prospect of impressive progress through DOTS expansion, some challenges remain. The treatment success rate is very high at 96 percent, but despite good progress in 2003 the case detection rate (45 percent) is still far from the 70 percent target (see table). Lack of staff, properly functioning dispensaries, and effective coordination between hospitals and the national TB program have been barriers to case detection, even within DOTS areas.

Indicators of progress against TB in China

Indicator	Coverage rate
DOTS population coverage, 2002	78 percent
Treatment success, 2001 cohort	96 percent
DOTS detection rate, 2002	27 percent
Prevalence (sputum smear positive per 100,000 population)	107
TB mortality per 100,000 population	21
Government contribution to total TB control cost, 2003	77 percent
Government health spending used for TB, 2003	0.3 percent

A World Health Organization report (WHO 2004j) identified several key remedial actions needed in China's program:

- Evaluate political commitment, implementation of national TB control plan, and funding needed and available at lower government levels.
- Hire experienced staff, enhance training through proposed DOTS training site, and revise/develop the Human Resource Development Plan.
- Test new approaches to strengthening hospital dispensary collaboration.
- Provide essential equipment and vehicles in impoverished areas.
- Develop strategies to strengthen multisectoral response to TB.
- Strengthen National Tuberculosis Control Program monitoring and evaluation system.

Figure 2.1

Trends in TB case notifications, selected regions, 1981–2002

Standardized notification rates

Note: Selections in each region are those for which case notifications were judged to represent trends in incidence from 1981 to 2002. To highlight trends in notifications within regions, the rates have been expressed relative to an arbitrary standard of 100 in 1990. Error bars are 95 percent confidence intervals on the standardized (unweighted) rates.

Established market economies: Australia, Austria, Belgium, Canada, Czech Republic, Denmark, Finland, France, Germany, Greece, Iceland, Ireland, Japan, Luxembourg, Netherlands, New Zealand, Norway, Portugal, Singapore, Spain, Sweden, Switzerland, United Kingdom, United States. *Central Europe:* Albania, Croatia, Cyprus, Hungary, Poland, Serbia and Montenegro, Slovakia, Slovenia, Turkey. *Eastern Europe:* Armenia, Bulgaria, Estonia, Kazakhstan, Kyrgystan, Latvia, Lithuania, Moldova, Romania, Russian Federation, Tajikistan, Turkmenistan, Ukraine, Uzbekistan. *Eastern Mediterranean:* Iran, Jordan, Lebanon, Morocco, Oman, Qatar, Saudi Arabia, Syria, Tunisia. *Latin America:* Argentina, Bolivia, Brazil, Chile, Cuba, Dominican Republic, El Salvador, Guatemala, Guyana, Honduras, Jamaica, Nicargua, Paraguay, Peru, Puerto Rico, Uruguay, Venezuela. *Western Pacific:* Hong Kong, China (SAR), Lao PDR, Macao, China (SAR), Malaysia, Republic of Korea, Viet Nam. *Southeast Asia:* Bhutan, India, Maldives. *Africa, low HIV:* Algeria, Benin, Comoros, Ghana, Guinea, Madagascar, Mali, Mauritania, Mauritius. *Africa, high HIV:* Botswana, Côte d'Ivoire, Democratic Republic of Congo, Kenya, Lesotho, Malawi, Uganda, Tanzania, Zambia, Zimbabwe.

Source: WHO 2004j.

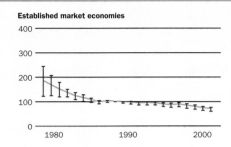
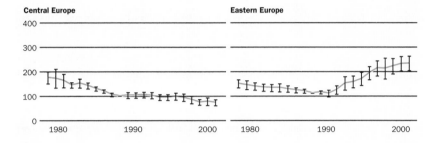
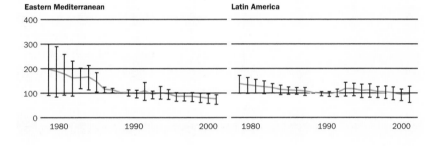
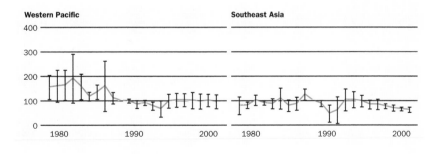
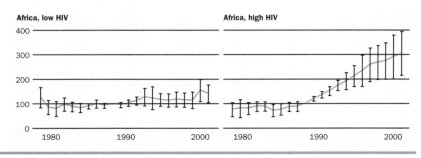

HIV infection massively increases the demands on TB programs

Worldwide in 2000, 11 percent of all new TB cases in adults (612,000) occurred in people infected with HIV, and 9 percent of all new TB cases were directly attributable to HIV.

But global figures mask extreme differences in national prevalence rates of HIV infection in new TB cases. Some countries (Afghanistan, Bangladesh, China, and Indonesia) had a rate under 1 percent. In others (South Africa and Zimbabwe), the rate was 60 percent or more. In all, it is estimated that some 11 million adults were co-infected with both TB and HIV—2 million in South Africa alone. The study from which these figures are taken calculated that almost a third of adult TB cases were attributable to HIV in the entire African region (Corbett and others 2003).

An HIV epidemic can lead to dramatic increases in the number of people who contract TB, even in countries that have traditionally had a low incidence of the disease. For example, in the United States just over a quarter of TB cases were estimated to be attributable to HIV (Corbett and others 2003).

There is a similar, mutually destructive, picture in relation to deaths. Globally, 12 percent (226,000) of all deaths from TB in 2000 were among HIV-positive people. Death rates reported for patients treated for HIV-associated TB are high, and may actually be even higher than reported since it is possible that fewer than half the fatal TB cases are diagnosed before death. Although TB is preventable and treatable, it is one of the most common causes of morbidity and death in HIV-positive adults living in developing countries.

This desperate situation poses some real challenges. Most of the recent successes in TB control have been in countries with low rates of HIV infection such as China, Peru, and Viet Nam. The task is much more difficult in high-prevalence HIV/AIDS settings.

HIV infection massively increases the demands on TB programs, which are struggling to cope with the increased TB caseload. The impact of HIV exposes any weaknesses in TB control programs. The rise in the number of people potentially ill with TB and needing to be tested is putting a strain on diagnostic services, and current TB diagnostic tools are less reliable in HIV-negative patients, with studies showing that the smear microscopy test detects pulmonary TB in only 35–38 percent of HIV-negative patients. Clinical diagnosis of TB is more difficult in co-infected patients, since similar symptoms can be caused by various infections.

Extrapulmonary and smear-negative pulmonary TB cases, which are more difficult to diagnose, account for an increased proportion of total cases. The diagnosis of TB in young children has always been difficult; it is even more so with HIV. There is a higher morbidity and mortality, partly due to other, curable, HIV-related infections. The risk of TB recurrence is higher. This catalogue of clinical, technical, and operational problems collectively poses a major challenge to ensuring that every individual in need gets appropriate diagnosis and treatment.

Reversing the incidence of TB will require an expanded strategy

Another key hurdle is the challenge of simultaneously administering anti-TB and anti-HIV treatments due to dangerous drug-drug interactions between rifampicin, a cornerstone TB drug, and most antiretrovirals. WHO guidelines indicate options for when someone receiving anti-TB treatment should start anti-HIV treatment and for selecting the appropriate anti-HIV treatment regimen. Preventive treatment of latent TB among HIV-infected people may to some extent limit the numbers of HIV-infected people who develop TB and therefore will need consideration of simultaneous anti-TB and anti-HIV treatments. The progress report on the Global Plan to Stop TB and other analyses have emphasized the need for new anti-TB drugs that are more compatible with antiretroviral treatment (Stop TB Partnership/WHO 2004, RESULTS 2004).

In addition to meeting the targets for TB case detection and treatment success, reversing the incidence of TB will require an expanded strategy with further measures in countries with a heavy burden of HIV. A recent paper from WHO and the Stop TB Partnership (Elzinga and others 2004) noted that in high-HIV populations—for example, in many countries in eastern and southern Africa—the incidence of TB is increasing at 10 percent per year without full implementation of the DOTS strategy. The paper argues on the basis of modeling that achieving the targets of 70 percent case detection and 85 percent cure rate would only slow down the rate of TB increase to 7 percent per year in these situations. Measures to implement the DOTS strategy fully—that is, improving its quality of delivery and engaging all heath providers—would not alone reverse the HIV-driven increase in TB.

By contrast, in the countries of the former Soviet Union where HIV prevalence was less than 1 percent in 2000, the model predicted that achieving the 2005 global case detection and cure rate targets would reverse trends rapidly—from a 10 percent annual increase in incidence to a 4 percent annual decrease.

DOTS is, at the present time, the most effective large-scale strategy for the treatment of TB. However, neither TB nor the challenges it presents have remained static. The need to evaluate and modify diagnostic and treatment protocols to address the changing features of the epidemic will continue to be a feature of the global response.

Today, one of the greatest challenges is the control of TB in settings where a large number of people have latent TB infection and there is a simultaneous burden of high HIV prevalence. Interventions to address these difficulties are all available, affordable, and incorporated in WHO's *Strategic Framework to Decrease the Burden of TB/HIV* and WHO's *Interim Policy on Collaborative TB/HIV Program Activities* (WHO 2002a, 2004a). There is consensus that controlling HIV-related TB requires an expanded strategy, consisting of measures taken directly against TB (full implementation of the DOTS strategy with intensified case-finding and preventive treatment) and measures taken

As of 2003, none of the 22 high-burden countries had implemented collaborative TB/HIV activities on a national scale

against HIV, and therefore indirectly against TB (HIV prevention, treatment of other HIV-related diseases, and HIV treatment).

An assessment carried out in October 2003 indicated that the key recommended interventions were so far being carried out on only a small scale (WHO 2004j). None of the 22 high-burden countries had implemented any collaborative TB/HIV activities on a national scale, though 15 have joint coordinating bodies and 12 carry out small-scale joint TB/HIV planning activities. The majority neither routinely tested TB patients for HIV, nor actively looked for TB among people infected with HIV. Few offered isoniazid preventive therapy, which WHO sees as an integral part of the package of care for those with both TB and HIV. Indeed, serious implementation of isoniazid preventive therapy had not been achieved anywhere in high-HIV/low-income settings, despite its potential to save lives (WHO 2004d). And few provided antiretroviral therapy or offered more than a little additional care and support for TB patients infected with HIV.

WHO's 2004 *Global Tuberculosis Control Surveillance* report notes that some national tuberculosis programs require DOTS programs to perform more effectively before attention is paid to the TB/HIV interaction (WHO 2004j). However, meeting the case detection targets is unlikely without, for example, the systematic referral of people suspected of having TB from voluntary counseling and testing centers and from other centers that provide services for HIV/AIDS patients.

There is growing financing for TB and for HIV/AIDS programs but, within this, there needs to be strong support for fully financed joint efforts, not just parallel streams. Encouragingly, the Global Fund to Fight AIDS, Tuberculosis, and Malaria (GFATM) did note that its Round 4 applications, considered in June 2004, showed significantly more attention to TB issues in proposals on HIV/AIDS and to HIV-related issues in proposals on TB than in previous rounds (Global Fund 2004). Although there was only one integrated TB/HIV application in Round 4 (which was unsuccessful), many successful TB proposals contained TB/HIV collaborative activities. Recognizing the need to address TB/HIV issues in both TB programs and HIV/AIDS programs, the GFATM will strongly encourage all HIV proposals to consider TB activities and all TB proposals to consider appropriate HIV activities in high-HIV prevalence settings. Fully exploited, GFATM grants for joint TB and HIV program activities should help to overcome the common problem of separate funding of TB and HIV programs, a barrier to their collaboration.

As described in the Kenya case study undertaken for this report (appendix 2), the Kenyan National Leprosy and TB Program is one of the few TB programs in the world that is administratively linked to the HIV/AIDS program. There is a joint plan to improve TB and HIV collaborative activities, including the referral of TB cases for HIV counseling and testing, the systematic screening of HIV-infected individuals for active TB, and the provision of isoniazid

Without the correct drugs, MDR-TB is untreatable

prophylaxis for those found to be infected with both diseases. Nonetheless, these remain largely plans and few activities have yet started.

Multidrug-resistant tuberculosis

In addition to HIV-associated TB, MDR-TB is an increasing threat.[3] WHO estimates that worldwide there are 300,000 new cases of MDR-TB each year, and it has now emerged in nearly every country of the world.

MDR-TB is TB that is resistant to at least the two most powerful drugs used to treat it, isoniazid and rifampicin. It can be transmitted from person to person but is fostered by poor prescribing by providers, low-quality first-line drugs, or irregular drug supplies that interrupt patient medication. Or patients may themselves simply stop taking the drugs, because they feel better, for example, or because the six- to eight-month course of treatment is so long and stressful.

Without the correct drugs, MDR-TB is untreatable and in most cases fatal. Access to second-line drugs is essential, but these are not available to most sufferers. Even when they are available, the course of treatment takes much longer (18–24 months), its efficacy is lower, and adverse reaction rates are higher. Though curing "normal" TB is cheap and effective—a six-month course of medicines costs $10—treating drug-resistant TB can be many times more expensive.

WHO and the International Union Against Tuberculosis and Lung Disease (IUATLD) operate a Global Project on Anti-tuberculosis Drug Resistance Surveillance, which reports on worldwide TB drug resistance at roughly three-year intervals. Their most recent (2004) report notes new evidence proving that drug-resistant strains are becoming more resistant and unresponsive to current treatments (WHO 2004b). Seventy-nine percent of MDR-TB cases are now "super strains," resistant to at least three of the four main drugs used to cure TB. With no effective vaccine, everyone is vulnerable to infection simply by breathing in a droplet carrying a virulent drug-resistant strain. And with no new drugs introduced in over 30 years, therapeutic options for treatment are increasingly limited, with the result that MDR-TB is often fatal.

The report also found that TB patients in parts of Eastern Europe and Central Asia are 10 times more likely to have MDR-TB than in the rest of the world. These populations are also facing the fastest growing HIV infection rates worldwide, compounding the challenges of TB control. Six of the top 10 global hotspots are Estonia, Kazakhstan, Latvia, Lithuania, parts of the Russian Federation, and Uzbekistan, with drug resistance in new patients as high as 14 percent. In two provinces in China, 1 in every 10 new patients tested positive for MDR-TB. Similarly high levels of resistance could exist elsewhere in China, since only 6 of the country's 23 provinces were represented in the study. Ecuador, Israel, and South Africa were also identified as key areas of MDR-TB.

The case of South Africa highlights the importance of high cure rates as an essential counterpart to better case finding. Of the countries most progressive in case detection, South Africa still reports a very low rate of treatment success (65 percent). Provincial surveys in 2001–02 found MDR-TB prevalence rates of up to 14 percent among previously treated patients. In at least one province, there were regular reports of drugs out of stock and high default rates from treatment, creating the conditions for increasing drug resistance. Each province has an MDR-TB treatment center, and in October 2003 South Africa had 4,000 MDR-TB patients on treatment with drugs costing an average of $3,400 per patient.

Africa and Central Europe reported the lowest median levels of drug resistance. Some successes have been achieved since the last study four years ago—most notably in Cuba, Hong Kong (China), and the United States, where rates have decreased as a result of strong and well maintained TB strategies. Earlier WHO/IUATLD reports in 1997 and 2001 concluded that good TB control practices are associated with lower or decreasing levels of resistance. The 2004 report of the Global Project on Anti-tuberculosis Drug Resistance Surveillance notes that TB control strategies used in Eastern Europe and the Russian Federation have recently begun to improve with the introduction of the DOTS strategy (WHO 2004b).

In the worst affected areas, innovative DOTS-Plus schemes are being introduced to diagnose and treat MDR-TB effectively. These schemes involve diagnosing MDR-TB through quality-assured culture and drug-susceptibility testing, and treating patients with second-line drugs under proper case management conditions.

Summary findings and conclusions

The summary findings and conclusions of the Working Group on TB are as follows:

Tuberculosis targets and current progress
- The Millennium Development Goals target for 2015 is to have halted, and begun to reverse, the incidence of TB. Its indicators are TB prevalence and death rates and the proportion of TB cases detected and cured under DOTS. In practice, the target should be to halve the prevalence of TB disease and deaths.
- Other targets have similar aims. Most notably, the World Health Assembly has process targets for 2005 of detecting 70 percent of new infectious cases of TB and successfully treating 85 percent of those detected.
- Globally, the incidence of TB continues to rise. This is largely due to its increased incidence in Sub-Saharan Africa, where HIV is a factor, and in the former Soviet Union, where drug resistance is a factor, compounded by collapse of the public health system and socioeconomic distress.

DOTS-Plus must be mainstreamed into countrywide TB control plans

The strategies to achieve the Millennium Development Goals target

- The basic platform for global TB control should remain full implementation of the DOTS strategy. This entails expanding DOTS to engage all TB care providers in delivering the international standard of TB care in line with DOTS, and to ensure that all patients have access to DOTS services.

- Rapid gains in case detection under DOTS by all providers could potentially be made in the Americas, Europe, and Southeast Asia. Even so, a radically different approach will be required to lift case detection rates from a likely plateau of 50 percent to the target of 70 percent. DOTS programs and public health authorities must work with non-participating providers to ensure they meet DOTS standards, especially those in the private sector in Asia and those outside the present limits of the public sector in Africa. These are the regions of the world that account for the vast majority of cases that are not yet detected by public health authorities.

- An 85 percent treatment success rate should be achievable on a global basis by 2005 or shortly after, though not in WHO's Africa or Europe regions.

- Modeling based on past experience suggests that achieving the twin targets of 70 percent case finding and 85 percent treatment success under DOTS should be sufficient to halt the incidence of TB—and achieve the Millennium Development Goals target—in countries with low rates of HIV infection, including those with high rates of MDR-TB.

- However, these measures will not alone reverse the HIV-driven increase in TB. Success on this front requires urgent action in affected countries to implement the adaptation of DOTS to HIV settings—an expanded and collaborative TB/HIV strategy, combining full implementation of the DOTS strategy with intensified TB case finding and treatment, the identification and treatment of latent TB in co-infected individuals, and HIV prevention and treatment. High cure rates for HIV-infected TB patients depend on improved national TB program performance, better access to antiretroviral therapy and cotrimoxazole preventive therapy, and better treatment of opportunistic infections. New, faster-acting drugs that are designed to be compatible with antiretroviral therapy are necessary.

- The emergence of MDR-TB requires the rapid expansion of patient access to appropriate treatment and second-line drugs in DOTS-Plus. DOTS-Plus must be mainstreamed into countrywide TB control plans.

- Success in achieving the Millennium Development Goals target should be measured by halting the incidence of TB in every region and country of the world, not just at a global level. A targeted strategy, reflecting regional and national characteristics, is essential. Sub-Saharan Africa

**An effective
vaccine that
works beyond
childhood and
in all settings
will represent
a crucial
breakthrough**

should be a special focus of international support, with exceptional measures to attack both poverty and TB/HIV co-infection.

A need for new tools

- Better, simpler, and more specific diagnostics are essential to speed case finding and identify TB in children and in high-risk populations, especially those already infected with HIV. Results known in minutes, not days or weeks, will offer a significant advantage in TB control.
- New drugs are needed to shorten and simplify treatment, overcome resistance, and ultimately treat latent infection to prevent transmission. When the current bane of treatment—its length and complexity—is dramatically improved, more patients will be treated, cure rates will increase, and resistance will be curtailed.
- Ultimately, an effective vaccine that works beyond childhood and in all settings will represent a crucial breakthrough in TB control. This is one of the most difficult, but rewarding, research and development efforts. Vaccines must be implemented alongside other new tools because of the challenges of addressing the one-third of the world's population that is already infected with TB.

Strategic priorities

- Overall, therefore, the focus of activities to meet the Millennium Development Goals target of reversing the incidence of TB should be on DOTS expansion; addressing TB and HIV/AIDS; mainstreaming DOTS-Plus for MDR-TB; and supporting the development of new diagnostics, new drugs, and new vaccines. This strategic focus is already the basis for the structure of the Stop TB Partnership, as outlined in the Global Plan to Stop TB, and is strongly commended by the UN Millennium Project Working Group on TB.

Chapter 3

Poverty, gender, children, and tuberculosis

Tuberculosis is a classic example of a social disease, characterized by its close correlation to socioeconomic conditions.

Poverty fosters tuberculosis

Airborne mycobacteria spread easily in overcrowded places and where other illnesses and poor nutrition reduce the immune defenses. This puts impoverished people at high risk of acquiring infection and developing active disease. Two centuries ago, the urbanization of many societies during the Industrial Revolution created the conditions for an explosive growth in TB incidence. This association between TB and the living conditions of the working poor and the destitute is still found today throughout the developing world.

The global and national distribution of TB correlates closely and inversely with national average per capita income. Low-income countries have a high incidence of TB and high-income countries have a low incidence (figure 3.1).

Resolving the global crises of acute poverty and inequality is clearly beyond the scope of any single disease control program. But the commitment to achieve the full range of the Millennium Development Goals presents an unprecedented opportunity for international cooperation and integrated action across sectors and interest groups. The TB community, for example, has a special interest in the Goal of eradicating extreme poverty and hunger—conditions that foster TB and that TB then fosters.

"Stop TB, Fight Poverty," the theme of the 2002 World TB Day two years ago, reflected the central importance of tackling poverty as a route to tackling TB. Since then, increasing prominence has been given to the need to target poor people in efforts to expand DOTS, and reaching out—within the health sector and beyond—to other public health practitioners, governments, and institutions working on poverty reduction strategies. Importantly, leaders in

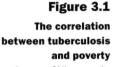

Figure 3.1

The correlation between tuberculosis and poverty

Average GNI per capita and average incidence of tuberculosis, 2000

Note: Countries are grouped by World Bank income/WHO tuberculosis incidence estimates for 2000.

Source: PIH 2004.

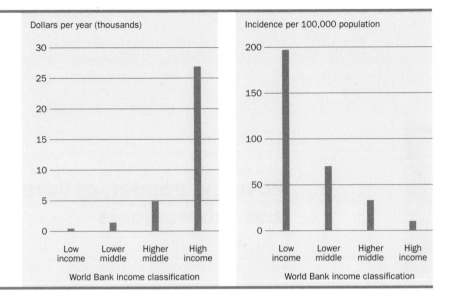

TB control and public health in some of the highest TB burden countries are committing to pay explicit attention to the needs of the poor in their operational strategies.

National TB programs rely on the full range of primary healthcare providers in public health clinics, hospitals, NGOs, private practice, community clinics, and the like to refer patients with symptoms that suggest TB for standardized diagnosis and treatment. But poor people—and other groups, including people in isolated rural communities, prisoners, refugees, the marginalized, the nomadic—often face serious financial, logistical, or political barriers to using health services. Thus there is a greater risk that their TB will not be diagnosed correctly or that they will start treatment late. Delayed treatment increases both the likelihood of death or permanent disability and the risk of transmitting the disease to others.

Within TB control, as across the spectrum of disease and illness, special efforts need to be focused on the most impoverished, vulnerable, and underserved populations. Programs must provide them with access to information, prevention interventions, diagnosis, and treatment. There is now growing evidence of significant socioeconomic differences within seemingly homogenous poor populations (Gwatkin 2003), so DOTS implementation must be designed to ensure that the poorest groups benefit fully. This is an area where further research is needed to monitor, evaluate, and recommend TB control approaches and tools aimed at enhancing equity.

Even with greater success on this front, cure of TB is not enough without tackling the desperate poverty in which it breeds. Box 3.1 has a powerful personal statement from Winstone Zulu, the well-known HIV/AIDS and TB service provider and activist. For some, being cured of TB means anxiety, not relief, when they are deprived of the TB program's food ration, and testing

Box 3.1

Poverty: a fate worse than tuberculosis or AIDS

Source: Winstone Zulu, Kara Counselling and Training Trust.

Jennifer Phiri looked vibrant compared with a year ago when she had started taking her TB drugs. Nine months later, tests showed her TB was cured effectively. She now sat in my small office at our HIV testing and counseling center, looking miserable and depressed.

Joyce Besa was in tears. She was 24 and very beautiful. She said her day-to-day living was made worse by the results of an HIV test earlier that day. She was found to be HIV-negative.

Why would anyone who receives the great news that their TB is cured be depressed?

Why would anyone who is told that he or she is HIV-negative be sad?

The day I learned the answer to these questions was the day I felt like resigning as an AIDS/TB service provider and activist. You see, I live in a town called Kabwe. Fifteen years ago it was a rich and vibrant place for its 300,000 people. Today Kabwe is a ghost town. Thousands lost their jobs when the mine closed in 1995, and thousands more were laid off by the railway headquarters. A mass exodus of people has left in search of greener pastures.

So when AIDS hit Kabwe, it was dealing a death blow to an already dying town. Children who were "economic orphans" became real orphans as their parents died from AIDS. Thousands of farm workers, in the only remaining form of employment, are getting sick and dying from AIDS. The road to the once-thriving "Copperbelt" is lined with sex workers selling their bodies for as little as a dollar per session.

It is in this environment that I was given the task of setting up an HIV/AIDS program by the Kara Counselling and Training Trust, a well established NGO that offers integrated psychosocial services among poor people in two other towns. We quickly set up a counseling and testing center in July of 2003. This was followed up by a hospice for the terminally ill, and then a street children's program. The voluntary counseling and testing program in Kara is not complete without solid support systems. These include a support group called Positive and Living Squads (PALS), which provides peer support and counseling for those who test positive. At a weekly group meeting, arts and crafts are designed and created, and members share their hopes and fears about the future. With money from the Stephen Lewis Foundation, 4,800 Kwacha is given as transport refund at the end of each meeting. This is roughly about 80 US cents per week per member.

The first meeting of the Kabwe PALS had 10 members. The following week we had 23 members and the third week an incredible 83. We were clearly heading for a budget overrun. So we decided to ask all the 83 members to test. Twenty-three were found positive. I was happy that only 23 were infected, as I feared for a worse figure.

The 60 people who were HIV-negative were not happy. Joyce was one of them. They wished they were HIV-positive so they could get the transport refund. The money is not used for transport but to buy food at home. Members walk long distances to come and get the few cents to help them sustain their lives. To be denied this money was worse than having AIDS.

Jennifer, sitting there in front of me, was complaining that now that her TB was cured, she would be removed from the list of patients who receive food packages of soya powder, cooking oil, and beans. She felt it would better to die of TB than starve to death. She said the food she received while sick was the only source of livelihood for her three children. Their father died of AIDS in 1988.

And here I am stuck with Jennifer and Joyce in my little office as they wish they had the most serious and fatal disease to have hit the world so they can get 80 cents every week. There are times when this planet looks so beautiful. There are times when one feels like migrating to some place elsewhere in the universe.

In a vicious circle, TB itself is a cause of poverty

negative for HIV means losing 80 cents a week to attend an HIV-positive peer support group.

Tuberculosis fosters poverty

In a vicious circle, TB itself is a cause of poverty. It imposes a severe economic burden on individual patients, their households, their health care systems, and their societies, mainly through the costs of diagnosis and treatment and the loss of income due to illness.

First, there are the direct costs, both for care and for accessing care. DOTS is an effective approach but it is also labor-intensive and expensive in terms of system costs. The cost of drugs to treat TB have decreased dramatically in recent years, but in those settings where people must pay for treatment, even the reduced cost can represent an impossible barrier for people living on less than a dollar a day. Patients and their families also often face significant additional costs—for travel, accommodation, and special nutrition during treatment. The substantial nontreatment costs borne by TB patients and their families are often greater than the costs of treatment borne by the health sector. In Zambia, researchers estimated these direct nonmedical costs incurred by TB patients were more than twice their medical costs (Needham, Godfrey-Faussett, and Foster 1998).

Second, because of the length of TB treatment, there are substantial indirect costs from lost production and lost income. Active TB is a debilitating illness that frequently causes prolonged absence from work and can result in loss of employment. Studies suggest that, on average, TB patients in developing countries lose three to four months work, resulting in lost potential earnings of 20–30 percent of annual household income. If the patient dies, their families lose an average of about 15 years of income. In India, researchers found that TB patients lost an average of 83 work days, with 48 days before treatment and 35 during treatment. Indirect costs represented 65 percent of these Indian families' costs for TB disease (Rajeswari and others 1999).

Although the aggregate real costs are higher for nonpoor patients, the relative costs for the poor are much higher. They have little disposable income because of the nature of their livelihood activities, such as daily wage labor and petty trading (Nhlema and others 2002). Periods of inability to work through ill health have a profoundly negative impact on employment and economic security, particularly for the self-employed and those working in the informal sector. In the absence of formalized laws that protect employment during serious and prolonged illness, even those with private sector jobs can find themselves out of work because of their illness.

Some coping strategies that households adopt to meet the costs of illness and death can have damaging long-term effects. In particular, selling family assets can reduce a household's economic prospects and incurring debt increases financial pressures. Reducing children's food intake or removing

TB is a top infectious killer of both men and women in their most productive years

them from school—to save fees or provide labor—can undermine their health, education, and future prospects.

Not all the costs are financial. TB patients and their families also pay the cost of TB in suffering, pain, and grief. TB has an impoverishing social impact. In certain societies, TB patients are seen as damaged for life or unmarriageable, and some may even be rejected by their families. This kind of stigma can result in anxiety, depression, and a general degradation of the quality of life.

Recommendations

- TB partners at all levels should strive to include TB in all antipoverty discussions and mechanisms. Most of the high-burden, least developed, and low-income countries do not include the impact of TB, nor do they target specific actions to control TB, in their poverty reduction strategies.
- In particular, national TB programs should be encouraged to address the links between TB and poverty in national guidelines and set the agenda politically, for example by advocating for the inclusion of TB control in official poverty reduction strategies. They should also welcome partners, such as NGOs, who can assist in providing the poor with services.
- DOTS programs must be flexible enough to meet the needs of patients who have special requirements or who live in particular conditions or geographical areas, especially the poor and vulnerable. TB partners should continue to find new ways to reach out to these patients such as community-based care, social support systems, and public-private models of service delivery.
- DOTS expansion should include equity initiatives in order to ensure that, even among the poor, the less well-off benefit as much as the better-off. DOTS strategy outcome measures should include appropriate indicators.
- Further research is needed to monitor, evaluate, and recommend refined TB control approaches designed to enhance equity and ensure equal access to services.
- Investment in novel R&D efforts to secure new, shorter, and affordable TB diagnosis and treatment is urgently needed in order to reduce the economic and personal costs to patients, their families, and society as a whole.

Tuberculosis and gender

TB is a top infectious killer of both men and women in their most productive adult years. Globally, males account for 60 percent of TB deaths and females for 40 percent. The burden of death among girls and women is great, at approximately 700,000 per year, and is of a similar magnitude to deaths due to maternal causes. According to TB case notifications reported to WHO, about twice as many men as women were notified that they had TB (WHO 2004j).

Studies suggest TB progresses from infection to active disease more rapidly in women of reproductive age

Prevalence surveys show that both the prevalence of infection with the bacillus that causes TB (*Mycobacterium tuberculosis*) as well as active TB disease is comparable between males and females until around age 15. However, a gender disparity with a rising rate among males emerges in late childhood and early adulthood and increases throughout most adult years, until it declines in old age.

Studies suggest that, given infection, TB progresses from infection to active disease more rapidly in women of reproductive age than in similarly aged men. Evidence of the impact of pregnancy on TB is inconclusive. However, it is clear that TB in pregnancy increases the risk of a poor pregnancy outcome. Case-control studies from Mexico and India report that pulmonary TB in a mother increases the risk of prematurity and low birthweight in neonates twofold, and the risk of perinatal deaths between three- and sixfold (WHO 2004l). Pregnant women with a late diagnosis of pulmonary TB also face higher risks of obstetric morbidity, miscarriage, eclampsia, and intrapartum complications (WHO 2004l).

A sociocultural factor affecting exposure may be the difference in social mixing patterns in many societies. Postadolescent women are often more restricted in their range of social contact, whereas men, with a wider range of employment and social activity, may increase their risk of infection through greater exposure (Dolin 1998).

Gender differences in behavior may influence disease progression. For example, poor nutrition, smoking, and alcohol abuse may result in decreased immunity. A 15-year study of 280,000 subjects across all age groups in southern India found that the risk of progression from infection to disease for pulmonary TB was 8.6 percent among men and 3.1 percent among women. Virtually all the alcoholics and smokers in the study population were men. After excluding smokers and alcoholics, the male-female ratio fell from 2.7:1 to 1.2:1 (WHO 2004l).

There are notable geographical variations in notification rates between men and women. These probably relate to a varying array of biological, socio-economic, and health service factors that affect exposure, infection, and illness onset as well as access to and use of services. A review of the current 20 high-burden countries that report notification by age and sex shows variations between countries. For example, Afghanistan reports higher notification rates in women of all ages. In Pakistan, rates between men and women remain essentially the same until around age 45, when men begin to outnumber women. Indonesia's notification rate remains equal until age 25. In other countries (Brazil, China, and Russia), from age 15 onward, case notification rates are much higher among men (WHO 2004j).

The current profiles of high-burden countries in Sub-Saharan Africa show consistently higher rates overall in men. However, with the exception of Tanzania, the gender ratio remains essentially the same (and in the cases of Nigeria

Women may delay longer in seeking care while men are less likely to complete treatment

and South Africa, women exceed men) at least until age 25 and in some cases until 35–40 (WHO 2004j).

Women ages 15–24 make up a higher proportion of TB cases in countries with higher rates of HIV infection (WHO 2004j). This fits with the observation that HIV prevalence tends to be higher in women than in men in this age range. As discussed earlier, HIV weakens the immune system and someone who is HIV positive as well as infected with TB is much more likely to develop active TB.

Gender differences in access to health care—and in preference for consulting private practitioners such as traditional healers, embarrassment, or fear of stigma—may be factors in differential case detection between men and women in some areas (Hudelson 1996). Studies have suggested that women may delay longer in seeking care for TB symptoms in a variety of settings, while men are less likely to complete treatment.

Both men and women suffering from TB can potentially experience devastating loss of income and social isolation. However, in many of the poorest, most heavily burdened countries, more women than men rely either on informal sector income or on the support of their partners. Many women may perceive social ostracism and the withdrawal of support by a partner and his family—where a diagnosis of TB in a woman is understood, among other features, as an indication of unsuitability for marriage—as a more immediately threatening prospect than TB itself.

Too little is understood about biological, socioeconomic, and health service factors affecting sex and gender differences in exposure, infection, illness onset, help-seeking, and utilization of services in TB control. This field of analysis is underdeveloped, but it has taken on more energy and importance as efforts expand and focus more on who is being missed and why.

Recommendations

- On current evidence, in most parts of the world, men face greater risks of TB than women, largely because of underlying biological factors and greater risk of exposure. Still, women fall ill and die due to TB in alarming numbers. If we aim to reduce gender differentials in development, then we need to address all important gender-related risk factors for disease or poor outcomes.
- As improvement in the welfare and development potential of women, especially in low-income settings, is a high priority, it will be important to examine underlying factors affecting either very large or very small gender-specific differences in case detection.
- In regions where TB-associated stigma for women is documented, it is urgent that health education and communication programs address this serious inhibitor to effective treatment and social well-being.
- As more information becomes available at the local and national levels documenting gender differences in TB disease and access to ser-

> **Children are particularly vulnerable to infection from household contacts**

vices, prevention and control strategies should be adapted accordingly. New community-based and public-private service models that aim to increase access and effective treatment, especially for those most vulnerable, should seek to address known gender-related barriers to care.

Tuberculosis and children

Childhood TB has been described as "a sentinel event in the community," as it usually indicates transmission from an (often undiagnosed or untreated) infectious adult (Shingadia and Novelli 2003). The risk for children in high-burden TB countries with large families and crowded living quarters is proven. Children are particularly vulnerable to infection from household contacts as they are often held, coughed and breathed on. An estimated 20–50 percent of children who live in households with active TB become secondarily infected (Stop TB Partnership 2004 website).

The current worldwide annual estimate of pediatric deaths due to TB is 450,000. In infants younger than one year, TB often progresses very rapidly, resulting in severe and disseminated disease. Without accessible health care, the disease is frequently fatal—fatal may be definitively diagnosed. Indeed, diagnosis itself is difficult. Tuberculin testing is often an inaccurate indicator of *M. tuberculosis* infection in young infants and those infected with HIV. Since most young children cannot cough up sputum, smear microscopy is usually not a relevant test. Detection rates in children with pulmonary TB through sputum microscopy are estimated at only 5 percent (MSF 2004).

TB in infants and children under age 16 has been a surprisingly underdeveloped area of research and attention. However, there has been recent movement toward better understanding and interventions in reporting and treatment of the disease in infancy and childhood (see, for example, Harries and others 2002). Under the auspices of the Global DOTS Expansion Working Group, a subgroup on childhood TB has now been formed.

Recommendations

• National TB programs should incorporate children with TB in all routine program operations.

• More work should be undertaken on diagnostic algorithms and the study of the epidemiology of childhood TB, especially in low-income settings where the burden is likely to be much higher.

• Operational approaches should be identified to enable health system workers to provide and maintain TB preventive treatment for children.

• BCG vaccine should continue to be promoted and made available for newborns, as part of the Expanded Program on Immunizations.

Investment is urgently needed to support the development of new, easy-to-use pediatric drug formulations and diagnostic tests that are effective in infants and children and appropriate for resource-poor settings.

Chapter 4

Moving forward to achieve the Millennium Development Goals target for tuberculosis

One of the great strengths of the campaign to halt the growth of tuberculosis (TB) is the high degree of consensus about the key targets, strategies, and constraints. There has been debate about an earlier focus on infectious sputum smear–positive cases (given limitations in capacity) rather than a universal approach of preventing or treating all cases of TB. But this has essentially been a debate about speed of progress, to allow for growth in capacity, rather than about principle. Action to achieve the target should now ensure that all TB patients have access to the universal standard of care based on the proper diagnosis, treatment, and reporting consistent with DOTS and its adaptations.

The key result areas are clear (box 4.1):

- Increasing DOTS coverage, participation, and quality, with improved case detection and cure rates.
- Adopting effective means to tackle HIV-related TB, with strengthened collaboration between TB and HIV/AIDS programs.
- Mainstreaming DOTS-Plus into DOTS to tackle multidrug-resistant tuberculosis (MDR-TB).
- Developing a complete set of new tools: new diagnostics, new drugs, and new vaccines.

Box 4.1

Key result areas

- Expand DOTS.
- Tackle TB/HIV effectively.
- Apply DOTS-Plus for multidrug-resistant tuberculosis (MDR-TB).
- Develop new diagnostics.
- Develop new drugs.
- Develop new vaccines

Effective liaison and collaboration among activities in these various areas is fundamental to success. Planning is already under way to integrate TB treatment with DOTS expansion plans, based on the success of DOTS-Plus pilots. The R&D and implementation communities must plan together to ensure that promising new products reach those in need as quickly as possible. The Stop TB Partnership has a vital role to play in providing the institutional mechanism for rapid sharing of information and fruitful collaboration.

Key intersections with other UN Millennium Project task forces

The global TB community must also reach out to other players and programs (table 4.1). The 2nd Ad Hoc Committee on the TB Epidemic (Stop TB Partnership/WHO 2004b) concluded last year that the main challenge for global TB control was expanding TB control activities across all healthcare providers and other stakeholders within the health sector, and across a broader range of stakeholders in sectors beyond health. In many countries, particularly in Sub-Saharan Africa, mutually beneficial cooperation between TB and HIV/AIDS programs will be crucial.

Table 4.1

Key intersections with other UN Millennium Project task forces

Sector	Intervention
Health	Controlling TB through universally implemented DOTS strategy and its adaptations where HIV or MDR-TB are common; support development of vaccines, new diagnostic tools, and new drugs.
	New and expanded primary services are needed, with a particular focus on poor people and geographically isolated communities.
Agriculture	Improved subsistence farming techniques improve nutritional outcomes for chronically malnourished populations and decrease vulnerability to TB.
Education	Education and literacy programs promote individual and collective empowerment and increase awareness of ways to prevent and treat a wide range of diseases, acute illnesses, and preventable injuries, including TB.
	Expanded access to higher education will increase the number of healthcare workers at all levels of care.
Gender equality	Women's empowerment leads to more informed and focused demand for available preventive and treatment options. Focused attention to reducing stigma and other socioeconomic barriers to care should improve outcomes.
Slum upgrading and urban planning	By eliminating overcrowded and poorly ventilated living and working spaces, vulnerability to TB is reduced.
	Slum upgrading and urban planning improve access to general health services and disease-specific interventions.
Science and technology	Research for the development of new drugs, vaccines, and diagnostics is needed to advance an effective response to TB.
	Improved communication technology can facilitate patient referral, disease surveillance, and control.
Energy	Reliable, sustainable, and modern energy services simplify and greatly improve the quality of diagnostic and treatment services across the healthcare spectrum.
Transport	Improved transport infrastructure reduces the distribution costs of drugs and critical supplies (such as diagnostic supplies). Improved geographic access, especially in isolated rural areas, will facilitate access to care and complete treatment.
	Improved transport infrastructure can facilitate movement of healthcare workers and reduce systemic obstacles to working in rural areas.

Box 4.2 **UN Millennium Project Working Group on TB recommendations**	• Ensure access for all to high-quality TB treatment. • Address the TB/HIV emergency now. • Engage all primary care providers in high-quality TB care. • Partner with communities in the effort to stop TB. • Stop the spread of MDR-TB. • Accelerate the development of critically needed new tools. • Support the Global Plan to Stop TB.

More broadly, progress in TB control both contributes to improved health and poverty reduction and also depends on progress in areas beyond TB. The 2nd Ad Hoc Committee therefore urged the TB constituency to work with the broader constituency of governments and agencies committed to accelerating health improvement and poverty reduction—just as this broader constituency should support TB control as part of its contribution to achieving the Millennium Development Goals. If the targets and Goals are to be achieved, the TB community must dramatically enlarge its current scope to address these issues effectively.

Solutions to constraints to improved tuberculosis control

The 2nd Ad Hoc Committee's extensive review of progress in implementing TB control was very opportune for this working group's current work on how best to achieve the Millennium Development Goals target for TB. The Committee was established on an ad hoc basis in 2003, under the auspices of the DOTS Expansion Working Group of the Stop TB Partnership, and contained representatives from governments, TB control implementers, disease control experts, and financing partners. As part of its task to examine constraints and solutions, it undertook a series of detailed consultations, so its findings have the benefit of drawing on a wide range of experience and views. Its report has been accepted by the Stop TB Partnership's board.

The UN Millennium Project Working Group on TB fully endorses the work of the 2nd Ad Hoc Committee and has built on this work in framing its own recommendations to scale up key TB control interventions, reach the poor, improve TB control tools, and achieve the Millennium Development Goals target by halving TB prevalence and deaths from 1990 to 2015 (box 4.2).

Recommendation 1: ensure access for all to high-quality tuberculosis care

All TB patients should have access to the universal standard of care that is based on proper diagnosis, treatment, and reporting consistent with the DOTS strategy. Providing people who need TB diagnosis and treatment with hugely expanded access to quality treatment under DOTS is an immediate necessity.

Scaling up TB control should build on improvements in health systems

Rationale

The basic pillars of a successful approach to achieving the target of halving TB prevalence and deaths by 2015 are understood, agreed upon, and in many cases already in place. These include structures, strategies, and supplies. New structures for improving global TB control include the Stop TB Partnership and its expert working groups, the Global Drug Facility (GDF), and the Green Light Committee. The DOTS strategy—combining political and patient commitment with a high-quality technical approach—has a proven track record of success. It has been adapted as DOTS-Plus to meet the challenge of treating MDR-TB, and an expanded strategy has been developed to tackle HIV-related TB (see appendix 1 for brief summaries of DOTS and its adaptations).

Although a lot has been achieved, and recent acceleration in access to DOTS quality care is encouraging, there is still a long way to go to achieve the targets.

It is crucial to act now to increase the scope, quality, and impact of the key TB interventions. This requires concerted action on several fronts: national action, international coordination, and innovative support mechanisms. Advocacy and political support will have a critical role to play.

Technically, the massive drive required to ensure that every person with TB has access to an effective DOTS program depends on consolidating and sustaining gains achieved so far, improving DOTS coverage and treatment success rates, and mainstreaming the adapted strategies to combat HIV-related TB and MDR-TB.

Those involved in DOTS implementation must engage more actively with broad health sector issues and health system strengthening. Scaling up TB control should build on and contribute to improvements in health systems—improvements that are critically needed. Five of the top six constraints reported by the TB high-burden countries are about health systems weaknesses, with inadequate infrastructure, weak laboratories, and poor monitoring and evaluation taking their place alongside lack of qualified staff and lack of capacity at peripheral levels.

TB programs alone cannot resolve the full range of these critical bottlenecks. Nonetheless, implementing DOTS can help strengthen health systems, for example through improved laboratory capacity (since microscopists provide a diagnostic service for diseases other than TB), improved documentation of health outcomes (through the TB recording and reporting system), and the potential for improved health management systems using the DOTS strategy as a model for a results-oriented health intervention.

Consistent drug supply is still an issue in many countries. Although the Global Drug Facility has been rightly acclaimed for ensuring enhanced flows of anti-TB drugs to poor countries, its work has been hampered by moments of acute financial stress—in 2003 it even considered temporarily scaling back its operations. It needs a longer-term assurance of funding than it has had so far. Countries embarking on rapid roll-out of DOTS programs and its adaptations

Lack of qualified staff was seen as by far the greatest constraint

must be confident that they will receive the predictable, sustained support they need to deliver the targets.

Among the TB high-burden countries in 2004, lack of qualified staff was seen as by far the greatest constraint to reaching the targets for case detection and cure. The underlying causes of the current human resource crisis are complex and rarely susceptible to quick fixes. They include financial and administrative barriers to creating and filling posts; stagnant employment mechanisms; an unhealthy work environment; HIV-related illness and death among health-care workers in high-HIV countries; and inadequate training, pay, conditions of service, and career opportunities. These broader health workforce problems cannot be solved by one disease program alone.

TB program action to broaden human resources for health includes mobilizing primary health centers and community-based providers to increase case-finding, identify cases earlier, and provide treatment support. Other recommendations already adopted by the Stop TB Partnership include promoting the development of sustainable institutional and individual capacity. Although many national TB program personnel and others involved in TB control at different levels exercise considerable managerial responsibilities, few have had the opportunity to acquire managerial expertise through formal training. More rigorous development of managerial capability among these personnel would help boost the quality of managerial performance (Ad Hoc Committee on the TB Epidemic 2003). Although there is growing recognition of the importance of training and human resource development as an integral part of national TB program activities, there has been little progress in finding ways to counter the loss of healthcare staff involved in organizing and delivering TB care in many developing countries.

Strengthening monitoring and evaluation is another key need. An accurate system of routinely reporting on TB cases and deaths (with national compilations every 3–12 months) is the ultimate tool for monitoring epidemiological trends and the impact of control measures. It is the endpoint toward which all countries should be moving.

In the interim, while systems for routine surveillance are being expanded and strengthened, some countries may wish to carry out population-based surveys of the prevalence of disease (preferably) or infection. Such surveys are highly desirable in any country that has, or probably has:

- A high TB burden.
- A high HIV burden (because the effect of HIV on TB epidemiology is still not well known).
- Poor information on burden and trends.
- A good control program, where a survey gives a baseline for measuring impact.
- In-country experience and expertise in the conduct of surveys.
- Adequate funding.

**All TB
patients
should have
access to
the universal
standard
of care**

Recommendations

- All TB patients should have access to the universal standard of care that is based on proper diagnosis, treatment, and reporting consistent with the DOTS strategy. It is urgent that people needing TB diagnosis and treatment are provided with massively expanded access to quality care under DOTS and adapted strategies for HIV-related TB and MDR-TB.

- Bringing these activities to successful outcomes will require long-term commitment from national governments, donors, and the Stop TB Partnership in its broadest sense. The TB community should demonstrate to the donor community and TB-endemic countries the effectiveness and added value of the new Stop TB Partnership bodies and their products. It should use their initial successes to advocate for sustained support over the next 10 years in order to achieve the Millennium Development Goals target by 2015.

- Scaled-up TB control at national level should build on and contribute to improvements in health systems. However, wider action to strengthen health systems in general, and health staffing in particular, will be an imperative. The current weakness of health systems is a major constraint to expanding access to quality TB care.

- Countries should plan to develop systems for routine reporting on TB cases and death, and also on drug resistance. In the interim, population-based surveys of the prevalence of TB disease are recommended, especially in countries with high TB or HIV burdens.

Recommendation 2: address the TB/HIV emergency now

"We cannot win the battle against AIDS if we do not also fight TB. TB is too often a death sentence for people with AIDS. It does not have to be this way. We have known how to cure TB for more than 50 years. What we have lacked is the will and the resources to quickly diagnose people with TB and get them the treatment they need."

—Nelson Mandela, July 15, 2004

Rationale

Along with the lack of universal implementation, availability, and use of DOTS, the HIV pandemic is one of the main reasons for continuing increases in TB burden.

The unprecedented scale of the epidemic of HIV-related TB demands effective and urgent action. At present, the highest numbers of TB/HIV co-infected individuals are found in developing countries, particularly in Sub-Saharan Africa, with growing incidence also found in some countries of the former Soviet Union and in East and South Asia. The deadly interaction of

HIV-related TB demands effective and urgent action

the TB and HIV epidemics feeds on and intensifies underlying conditions of poverty and social exclusion.

Unless HIV is controlled, TB will continue increasing wherever these epidemics overlap. Unless TB is controlled, people with HIV will continue falling sick and dying from a preventable, curable disease. The strategic goal is to reduce TB transmission, morbidity, and mortality (while minimizing the risk of anti-TB drug resistance), as part of overall efforts to reduce HIV-related morbidity and mortality in high-HIV populations.

There is increasing recognition that:

- TB is one of the leading causes of HIV-related morbidity and mortality.
- HIV is fueling the TB epidemic in high-HIV populations.

Tackling TB should include tackling HIV as the most potent force driving the TB epidemic; tackling HIV should include tackling TB as a leading killer of people living with HIV/AIDS. TB programs and HIV programs are thus interdependent and must collaborate at all levels from global policy to national planning and service delivery at the local level. This collaboration should support a strengthened health sector approach to control TB among HIV-infected people.

As noted earlier in this report, achieving the Millennium Development Goals target of reversing the HIV-driven increase in TB requires not only full implementation of the DOTS strategy but also additional measures. TB control in populations with high HIV prevalence requires a new expanded strategy:

- Interventions against TB: full implementation of the DOTS strategy with intensified case-finding and TB preventive treatment.
- Interventions against HIV, and therefore indirectly against TB: for example, the use of condoms, treatment of sexually transmitted infections, and antiretroviral treatment (WHO 2004a, c).

It is no longer acceptable for TB programs and HIV/AIDS programs to continue pursuing largely separate courses; they need to collaborate to exploit synergies in supporting health service providers to deliver these interventions (Dermot Maher, personal communication, 2004). Collaboration has the potential to yield efficiencies in surveillance, case detection, patient counseling and support, preventive therapy and treatment of disease, procurement of drugs and supplies, program management and, most importantly, treatment outcomes. TB/HIV collaboration has already led to progress in the management of both diseases. There is recognition of the differences in clinical presentation and treatment outcomes of HIV-related and of non-HIV-related TB, and therefore, for example, the need for more attention to sputum smear–negative pulmonary TB. The requirements are becoming increasingly clear for scaling up the use of isoniazid preventive therapy, cotrimoxazole preventive therapy, and antiretroviral therapy.

WHO's "Interim Policy on Collaborative TB/HIV Activities" (WHO 2004a) provides guidelines that define specific activities to address the dual epidemics (box 4.3).

Box 4.3

World Health Organization–recommended TB/HIV collaborative activities

Source: Adapted from WHO 2004a.

A. Establish the mechanisms for collaboration.
  A.1   Set up a coordinating body for TB/HIV activities effective at all levels.
  A.2   Conduct surveillance of HIV prevalence among TB patients.
  A.3   Carry out joint TB/HIV planning.
  A.4   Conduct monitoring and evaluation.
B. Decrease the burden of TB in people living with HIV/AIDS.
  B.1   Establish intensified TB case finding.
  B.2   Introduce isoniazid preventive therapy.
  B.3   Ensure TB infection control in healthcare and congregate settings.
C. Decrease the burden of HIV in TB patients.
  C.1   Provide HIV testing and counseling.
  C.2   Introduce HIV prevention methods.
  C.3   Introduce co-trimoxazole preventive therapy.
  C.4   Ensure HIV/AIDS care and support.
  C.5   Introduce antiretroviral therapy.

Aims described in that interim policy include:

- Reducing TB incidence among people living with HIV/AIDS—through collaborative efforts to improve the performance of national TB programs, through isoniazid preventive therapy for co-infected patients, and through earlier detection of active TB through intensified case-finding.
- Reducing HIV incidence and disease among TB patients—through voluntary counseling and testing for people at risk of HIV and preventive methods and therapy.
- Improving the care of people who are infected with both TB and HIV—through cross-training and collaborative care initiatives.

These and other interventions require that health ministries in high-burden countries have leadership, technical assistance, resources, and trained staff to provide HIV testing and counseling, TB treatment services that can cure a high proportion of cases, and teams that can link HIV care and TB control services in novel and effective ways.

A key element will be the rapid expansion of voluntary HIV testing and counseling in existing TB treatment programs, including diagnostic and routine testing and counseling (WHO 2004d).

At the same time, TB case-finding efforts in high-HIV prevalence settings will be intensified. Through cross-training, TB health workers will assist in HIV prevention, antiretroviral medication distribution, and patient care.

By encouraging programs providing antiretrovirals to utilize the lessons learned from TB program experience and, in turn, by utilizing successful HIV program experience in social mobilization and advocacy within national TB programs, both programs will be enhanced, providing expanded outreach and services to patients.

**Operational
research must
be intensified**

One continuing area of concern is that existing TB drugs and diagnostics are faring poorly in the battle against HIV/AIDS. Although sputum-smear microscopy detects the infectious TB cases, new diagnostics are needed to improve detection of the noninfectious TB cases. New diagnostics are also needed for earlier diagnosis, since late diagnosis causes life-threatening disease and unnecessary early TB or AIDS mortality. The development of a new, more reliable screening test for latent TB would be particularly helpful. Since interactions between anti-TB and antiretroviral drugs complicate their simultaneous use in treating HIV-infected TB patients, operational research is needed to evaluate current guidelines (WHO 2003a, c). The development of new drugs with fewer interactions would facilitate the simultaneous use of anti-TB and antiretroviral drugs.

Recommendations

- TB and HIV/AIDS partnerships must urgently step up collaboration at the global, national, and service delivery levels to deliver an expanded DOTS strategy to control HIV-related TB. This strategy consists of measures to attack both TB (full implementation of the DOTS strategy with intensified case-finding and preventive treatment) and HIV—and therefore indirectly TB (including prevention of HIV transmission and provision of cotrimoxazole and antiretrovirals).
- Countries and donors must specifically focus on combating the TB/HIV emergency. Tackling the immediate crisis requires an urgent and exceptional effort to maximize the benefit of current levels of funding and support from the international community. Work is now in hand to quantify the increased levels of support needed to meet the Millennium Development Goals target.
- The expanded DOTS strategy to control HIV-related TB will be successful only through patient-centered, countrywide TB and HIV collaborative service delivery.
- Increased priority must be given to the development of drugs, diagnostics, and vaccines that are reliable in HIV-infected TB patients. This includes drugs that are compatible with antiretroviral treatment.
- Operational research must be intensified to define the best strategies for joint management of the overlapping epidemics, including effective program collaboration at all levels to improve performance of both TB and HIV programs.

Recommendation 3: engage all primary care providers in high-quality TB care

TB control depends on effective diagnosis, treatment, and follow-up, mainly in primary care.

Faster progress in global TB control and care will entail involving all care providers

Rationale

Faster progress in global TB control and care will entail involving *all* care providers, both public and private, in delivering the same high standard of care and support to all TB patients.

Expanding the reach of the DOTS strategy, while mainstreaming effective TB/HIV linked interventions and DOTS-Plus for MDR-TB, requires implementing current policy guidelines on the contributions of all providers.

Decentralization. The dramatic HIV-driven increase in the TB caseload has greatly increased the pressure on existing government health service providers. This has prompted growing recognition of the need to promote the decentralization of national TB program activities from hospitals to primary care facilities, including their integration with the activities of all general health service providers at the district level. In some programs, the usual policy is to hospitalize TB patients during the initial phase of treatment, with ambulatory treatment during the continuation phase. Decentralization, with ambulatory treatment at a facility as close as possible to the patient's home, provides patients with easier access to care. It could also ease pressure on hospitals, especially in settings struggling with high numbers of HIV patients.

Alongside decentralizing service delivery, decentralizing health system management and financing continues to be a challenge, even in some countries where it has been under way for years. The technical support that would enable staff at provincial and district levels successfully to assume their new responsibilities has not been adequately planned for or provided. Afghanistan, Bangladesh, Cambodia, Kenya, Mozambique, Myanmar, and Pakistan all report having staff with inadequate qualifications working at the peripheral level. This points to the need for much greater planning and support for decentralization.

Private practitioners. Despite the presence of an effective low-cost or free national TB program, a significant number of TB patients opt for treatment by private practitioners. In India, the private sector is believed to manage half of all TB cases. That some people assume significant debt to obtain private treatment available to them free of charge under a government-sponsored national TB treatment program is a lesson about the power of popular perceptions of the public program. This behavior also draws attention to social dynamics associated with poverty, stigma, privacy, gender and ethnic disparities, and the complex relationships between physicians and their patients (Sykes, Tolhurst, and Squire 2003).

Meeting the DOTS targets and providing increased access to good-quality TB care therefore depends on two things. First is addressing the specific concerns that cause so many poor people to opt for private treatment. And second is engaging the full range of health providers under national TB program stewardship. This must cover government services, whether ministry of health (nationally and locally administered services) or not (for example, social security schemes, prisons, military), and nongovernment services, such as NGOs, community groups, private practitioners, and employers.

In practice, all health providers should either refer patients to public health facilities delivering TB care under the DOTS strategy or deliver TB care consistent with the DOTS strategy in collaboration with the national TB program. Governments should consider reform of legislative and regulatory frameworks to engage the full range of health providers and will need to invest in developing human resource capacity for strengthened national treatment program stewardship and service delivery.

Public-private mix projects. Since the beginning of 2001, the Stop TB Partnership has coordinated four public-private mix projects to explore innovative forms of partnerships. Robust and effective public-private mix DOTS models share the following features:

- Improved referral and information systems through simple practical tools as an essential component for the effective operationalization and evaluation of public-private mix projects. Training to ensure that national treatment program staff is sensitized to the public-private mix philosophy, and private providers to the DOTS philosophy.
- Sufficient supervision and monitoring of private providers by the government sector.
- Drugs free of charge to patients to improve treatment outcome, promote equity, and also provide a tool for steering private providers through formal or informal "drugs for performance contracts."
- In the case of the nonpoor, prepayment plans as an alternative to free drugs.

The business sector. To date, there have been only small-scale efforts to involve the business sector (that is, public and private sector organizations and enterprises) in TB control. Yet there are several complementary ways these organizations can contribute, including by providing:

- Expertise in management, communication, and innovative social mobilization techniques and country-specific knowledge.
- Means to reach some TB patients not easily covered by the public health system through workplace and related infrastructure, including employees and their families and remote or rural communities surrounding large business operations.
- In-kind and financial resources, including staff, products, and services, ranging from secondments to training, and from logistics support to medical supplies.

When companies are approached and supported with targeted tools (such as WHO and the International Labour Organization's "Guidelines for Work-

Delivery by all providers of care consistent with DOTS is crucial

place Control Activities" (WHO/ILO 2003), however, results have been very encouraging. Efforts should be scaled up by the TB community at large.

Recommendations

- Scaled-up TB control should be further integrated as a key component of primary care. TB control depends on effective TB diagnosis, treatment, and follow-up, mainly in primary care.
- National TB programs should engage the full range of public, private, and voluntary healthcare providers in TB control activities under their stewardship, with reform of legislative or regulatory provisions if necessary. The delivery by all providers of care consistent with the DOTS strategy as the internationally recommended standard is crucial to achievement of global TB targets.
- The same high standard of care and support should be provided to all TB patients.
- National TB programs should consider public-private mix approaches as a means to expand and strengthen DOTS, with an emphasis on improving case detection and treatment success.
- TB program managers should seek to include TB control measures in established business sector health activities, especially in HIV/AIDS programs. Government programs in high-burden countries should translate the global guidelines for managing TB at the workplace into local partnership tools to guide collaboration with the employers.

Scaling up the supply of effective TB services must go hand in hand with scaling up the demand for them.

Recommendation 4: partner with communities to stop tuberculosis

Scaling up the supply of effective TB services must go hand in hand with scaling up the demand for them.

Rationale

To date, government health service providers have been the main focus of TB control activities. Success in the future demands a broader approach. This includes more active partnership with communities. The community must be part of the solution to challenges in TB control (Stop TB Partnership/WHO 2004b). Securing effective collaboration with these new actors will require new ways of working—and differentiated ways of working, tailored to the specific needs of each group.

Community action for tuberculosis. One of the great challenges of the current global TB emergency is reaching the populations most vulnerable to infection with the information they need on how to recognize an active TB infection,

Donor and technical agencies should support countries in building capacity

on the treatment options available to them, and on organized ways for communities to advocate for treatment programs where they do not currently exist. Reports from some high-burden countries acknowledge the extent to which low public awareness and the stigma of having TB—and, for some people, HIV as well—hampers efforts to detect and treat TB suspects.

The stigma also hampers the growth of grassroots advocacy groups. Persistent public and behind-the-scenes pressure at national and local levels is needed to ensure that pledges are kept and appropriate policies are enacted. Ideally this popular pressure should be generated by the lobbying activities of TB interest groups within countries. Well organized activist groups for TB, however, remain rare. The people most afflicted by TB tend to be among the populations with the least visible presence within the institutions charged with the design and funding of these programs. Stigma and paradoxically the return to fully active, productive life following cure inhibit some sufferers from playing an active advocacy role.

The Stop TB movement needs to partner with whole communities, civil society groups, local NGOs, representatives of groups of TB patients and HIV activists, the local education sector, and local leadership at the grassroots to ensure that the poor and vulnerable are not missed. Through active recruitment and routine inclusion of community and grassroots organizations into the planning, implementation, and evaluation processes, national TB programs could be provided with essential local knowledge and experience.

The effectiveness of HIV/AIDS activists and community advocates in addressing both local and global AIDS issues is one notable example of the value of these approaches. Advocacy, care, and support from within the communities affected by HIV/AIDS can play a vital role in supporting earlier TB case detection, broader access to DOTS, and higher TB treatment completion rates. The key for national TB programs and other players will be to facilitate and support without undermining local ownership. Informed, local participation is the most direct way to address obstructive misconceptions and to facilitate educational outreach (box 4.4).

At the same time, TB programs need to take a more active and innovative approach to improving knowledge of TB symptoms and sources of help, particularly among the most poor and marginalized people. There is scope to learn from other programs (notably for HIV/AIDS), and to pilot TB-specific approaches to find out which are best for a given setting and which messages have the most impact. Appropriate communications and information strategies are vital. Brochures and posters are useful in literate communities that are seeking health information. But other tailored approaches are essential to engage the larger public. These include street rallies, speeches in places of worship, radio programs, television shows, and information at school and at work (box 4.5).

Donor and technical agencies should support countries in building capacity for advocacy, communications, and social mobilization at all levels as a

Box 4.4

**Community action
for tuberculosis
in Peru**

Source: Van der Linde
2003. Photograph
from Partners In Health
Archives.

*Tuberculosis patients and supporters
demonstrate in Lima*

In 1967, the first specialized division within the health ministry for the detection and treatment of TB (and leprosy) was formed in Peru. By 1976, with TB incidence continuing to grow, a concerted effort was begun by community activists to organize patients diagnosed with TB to demand better and expanded treatment as a basic human right.

By 1987 this movement was recognized on the national level. Even amid the political turmoil of that era in Peru, TB was officially recognized as a growing public health threat by the government and laws to mandate universal free treatment were enacted. The demonstrations and the formation of community support groups played an important role in shaping government policy and mobilizing effective strategies to overcome logistical barriers to treatment. As expressed by one of the community organizers, "The voice and presence of TB patients in society helps to create wider awareness about the complexity of TB and motivates the commitment of new actors in the fight."

By 2000, through the joint efforts of the patient organizations, the Peruvian Ministry of Health, and the international TB community, there was full DOTS program implementation in 99 percent of the health services throughout Peru and a scale up of a DOTS-Plus program. In 2001, Peru was the first country to be removed from the high-burden country classification.

routine part of DOTS expansion plans. Information systems should reflect this effort by developing and reporting indicators that can be utilized to monitor progress in these areas.

Seeking to mobilize support for disease-related programs can be met by the assertion of activists within impoverished communities that they suffer from other consequences of poverty that require more immediate attention, such as lack of adequate nutrition, drinking water, sanitation facilities, and safe housing. Starvation and near-starvation trumps most other needs in the short term, including the control of diseases, regardless of how clearly the diseases have been demonstrated to pose a profound global threat. Integrated action to secure the full suite of Millennium Development Goals will be key.

Community-based care. Using neighbors and associates of people diagnosed with TB, MDR-TB, and HIV/AIDS to provide supervised services such as medication administration, routine care, and assistance has proven helpful in many low-income settings. Infectious diseases such as TB and HIV/AIDS rarely have impacts on only one individual. The cost in terms of human and economic resources also has profound consequences for families and communities. So using community TB treatment supporters engages people who have a social and economic investment in improving the quality of life within their community.

Box 4.5	The use of the mass media in diagnosis and treatment outreach campaigns is a promising but underdeveloped focus of investigation. However, the best known, most evaluated tools of mass media—television, commercial radio, and newspapers—are not necessarily accessible to or targeted to deeply impoverished communities whose people often suffer from high illiteracy rates. Local programming in the form of community radio campaigns could prove an effective strategy to reach underserved populations. Although not found in every home, radios are often a feature of community gathering places in even the poorest, most rural communities. Because the station output strongly reflects the general knowledge, language, and issues of the community in which it is situated, focused educational campaigns targeted at radio station personnel could provide key information about diagnosis and treatment and contribute to the reduction of stigma. Operational research is needed to determine if community radio could be an effective tool in tuberculosis control.
The use of mass media in outreach campaigns: A case for research	

The model of directly observed treatment developed in the treatment of TB and home-based directly observed therapy for MDR-TB is now being adapted for antiretroviral therapy for people with HIV/AIDS (Farmer and others 2001). It is a cost-effective way to provide medicines and services that brings the added benefit of creating a supportive network for patients and their families (see, for example, Wilkinson and Davies 1997; Wilkinson 1999; Mitnick and others 2002). This becomes critically important in high disease–burden regions where the traditional support provided by extended families may be eroded by the death and disability of multiple family members.

In a review of eight "Community TB Care in Africa" projects in six countries, the investigators made the following recommendations (WHO 2003b):

- Extend TB care in the community to improve access.
- Identify suitable community TB treatment supporters in consultation with the community.
- Ensure that effective systems extend into the community for recording and reporting, and for the supply of anti-TB drugs.
- Monitor community contribution to TB care, using standard indicators.
- Develop costed plans for expansion of the community approach. Ministries of health should ensure adequate financing; coordinate the efforts of national TB programs, donors, and NGOs to ensure sustainability; and consider opportunities for collaboration between national TB programs and HIV/AIDS programs.

In regions hit hardest by the epidemics and experiencing a loss of health workers because they have relocated, emigrated, or are victims themselves, expanding the pool of paid community health workers may be the only immediately available option to support the development and expansion of diagnostic outreach and treatment programs.

It is critical to develop new anti-TB drugs

Recommendations

- National TB programs efforts should intensify efforts to partner with communities in tackling TB and responding to local needs. Potential partners include civil society groups, representatives of TB patients, the broad HIV/AIDS constituency, the local education sector, and local leadership at the grassroots level.
- Donor and technical agencies should support countries in building capacity for advocacy, communications, and social mobilization at all levels, as part of DOTS expansion plans, and in developing information systems that include indicators on advocacy, communication, and social mobilization. National TB programs should be supported in working with grassroots community groups as an essential part of the strategy to articulate demand for improved health care, including TB control.
- National TB programs should work to increase the use of community TB treatment supporters.

Recommendation 5: stop the spread of multidrug-resistant tuberculosis

The threat of MDR-TB is growing. Its emergence in nearly every country of the world holds the prospect of profoundly damaging consequences from an increasingly limited choice of therapeutic options in the face of "super strains" to the far greater difficulty and cost of treating patients with MDR-TB.

Rationale

Drug resistance needs to be tackled as swiftly and effectively as possible. There are three main streams of action, all of which are priorities.

First, it is essential that normal DOTS programs should be expanded and fully and effectively implemented, in order to minimize the conditions for further drug resistance to occur.

Second, treatment of MDR-TB requires that DOTS-Plus be scaled up and mainstreamed into countrywide TB control plans. This is a matter of special urgency in areas where MDR-TB rates are already serious. DOTS-Plus is an adaptation of DOTS, providing a programmatic approach to the diagnosis and treatment of MDR-TB within the context of DOTS programs (see appendix 1).

Third, it is critical to develop new anti-TB drugs, both to treat patients with MDR-TB and to minimize the emergence of new resistance.

Patient access to MDR-TB drugs is key to the success of the DOTS-Plus strategy. The Green Light Committee (GLC) was established in 2000 with the triple aims of preventing the misuse of second-line drugs, promoting access to quality-assured drugs, and providing technical assistance to countries implementing DOTS-Plus. After review by the GLC, successful applications for DOTS-Plus pilot projects can secure preferentially priced, second-line drugs.

The Green Light Committee is in critical need of financing to support technical assistance

The Committee has succeeded in negotiating price reductions of 95 percent for the most expensive regimens.

To date, the GLC is procuring drugs for and providing technical assistance to 25 DOTS-Plus projects, which are treating 8,200 people with MDR-TB. A further 8 projects, designed to treat 1,500 more patients, are being reviewed. However, in order to move forward, the GLC is in critical need of financing to support technical assistance to current projects and those under consideration.

The pace of enrollment is scaling up due to the endorsement of mainstreaming DOTS-Plus into DOTS by WHO and the TB international community, and to financial support from the Global Fund to fight AIDS, Tuberculosis, and Malaria (GFATM). The GFATM has selected the Green Light Committee as the mechanism for procuring and monitoring second-line drugs for MDR-TB. If projects submitted to the GFATM meet GLC requirements, the GFATM will support them financially. After its first four rounds of applications, the GFATM projects quadrupled MDR-TB treatment globally, with 12,000 new DOTS-Plus treatments for drug-resistant TB being provided by all GFATM-approved programs over five years (Global Fund 2004).

Recommendations

- Preventing MDR-TB should be tackled through full and effective implementation of DOTS, and treatment through scaled up DOTS-Plus programs, with special urgency in areas where MDR-TB rates are already serious. DOTS-Plus must be mainstreamed into countrywide control plans.
- Investment is needed to maintain financial support for existing second-line drugs and to develop new drugs. To treat MDR-TB there needs to be a pipeline of novel drugs, administered in combinations that will minimize the emergence of new resistances.
- Urgent support is needed for the Green Light Committee to allow them to provide technical assistance for programs wishing to implement and scale up DOTS-Plus.
- Drug resistance information should be monitored as an indicator of the quality of treatment programs. At the moment, testing TB patients for drug resistance—like testing patients for HIV—tends to be handled as a separate exercise, but the goal should be to incorporate both into routine case surveillance.

Recommendation 6: accelerate the development of critically needed new tools

Current diagnostics for TB are over 100 years old, no vaccine has come to market since the 1920s, and most of the drugs used to treat the disease are over 30 years old.

Technology exists that can vastly improve detection rates

Rationale

Investment in the development of new tools (diagnostics, drugs, and vaccines), followed by the rapid introduction of new tools in actual program activities, holds out the prospect of faster progress in TB control in future.

In each of the three tool areas, in addition to ongoing academic and government research, there is a new pathfinding research agency combining public and private approaches that is dedicated to developing affordable and better tools for use in TB high-burden environments. Initial support has come from several leading foundations and governments, especially the Bill and Melinda Gates Foundation and the Rockefeller Foundation.

In diagnostics, the nonprofit Foundation for Innovative New Diagnostics was created in 2003 to speed the development of improved diagnostic technologies, particularly for their effective and affordable use in high-burden countries. The recent momentum in drug development is being spearheaded by the Global Alliance for TB Drug Development (TB Alliance), a public-private partnership launched in 2000 that has developed the first pipeline of TB drugs in over 30 years. The agenda for vaccines, a longer term and important undertaking, is led by the Aeras Global TB Vaccine Foundation. Each of these bodies is a key partner in the respective new tool working group within the Stop TB Partnership. Further details of these agencies are given in appendix 6 of this report.

Although there are many examples of public-private partnerships to improve global health, one important feature of these new efforts is their single focus on product development by stimulating and ensuring a global pipeline for better diagnostics, drugs, or vaccines. A second feature is the nonprofit nature of the business model and its emphasis on the pricing of the end product, which must be affordable in order to reach patients and help overturn the trends of the epidemic. Third, these agencies emphasize the important contributions of public and private sectors and leverage the capacity, resources, and counsel of industry, the public health sector, and academic laboratories.

To maximize the success of these partnerships and ensure that end products reach patients in need, policymakers and public health officials should facilitate collaboration between these entities and their partners. Partners include the health and technology sectors of high-burden countries and pharmaceutical and biotechnology companies with relevant expertise and the resources and capacity to contribute. Initial forecasting estimates suggest the enormous synergistic impact of the three new tools. They highlight how the combined introduction of new diagnostics, drugs, and vaccines would dramatically improve TB control by:

- Enabling better detection and treatment of MDR-TB and TB/HIV.
- Expanding avenues of control to include sputum smear–negative cases.
- Overcoming latent infection through effective vaccines.

New diagnostics. At the present time, smear microscopy is the only technique available to diagnose TB in developing countries. Technology exists that can

Increased attention must be given to developing new diagnostics, drugs, and vaccines

vastly improve detection rates of TB, but this has been widely used only in affluent societies. Although smear microscopy requires minimal equipment, it is not highly reliable because it depends largely on the ability of patients (who may be too young, too debilitated, or simply unable) to produce an adequate specimen from the lower respiratory tract for examination. Also, increased attention must be given to the development of diagnostics (as well as drugs and vaccines) that are reliable in HIV-infected TB patients.

The standard for diagnosis of both TB and drug-resistant strains is a culture. Cultures are much more sensitive than smear microscopy, but they require weeks of incubation and careful, temperature-sensitive, light-sensitive, and time-sensitive chain-of-specimen handling from the patient to the laboratory. Reducing the length of time required to definitively diagnose TB or to identify drug-resistant strains—from several weeks to a matter of two to three days—promises to facilitate rapid diagnosis and the prompt initiation of treatment (creating, among other advantages, a decrease in the amount of time patients remain contagious to their close contacts). Public-private collaborations on TB diagnostics have yielded several promising possibilities currently in development that include improved, more rapid (sensitive) culture mediums and new tools. For example, Biotech Laboratories, in partnership with the Foundation for Innovative New Diagnostics (FIND), hopes to launch reliable, fast, low-cost, and easy-to-use products including a multidrug resistance test in early 2005 and a TB diagnostic tool by 2005–06.

New drugs. After several decades of standstill, a coordinated, global effort across public and private sectors to develop new, faster-acting drugs to improve TB control has helped yield the first comprehensive TB drug pipeline since the 1960s. The near-term prospect of simplifying or improving therapy is now a realistic possibility. Two fluoroquinolone drugs, moxifloxacin and gatifloxacin, are in Phase II clinical trials. A third drug, rifapentine, is in a sponsored study to examine its potential to shorten the treatment required for latent infection. Several compounds are in or approaching Phase I clinical trials. These drugs are being studied by sponsors as diverse as Lupin Laboratories, an Indian pharmaceutical company; Sequella, a small biotechnology company headquartered in Rockville, Maryland; and Tibotec, a subsidiary of the multinational pharmaceutical company Johnson & Johnson. The prospect of a novel treatment with a totally new drug is also represented by the family of the nitroimidazole compound PA-824 and its analogs, which are being developed by the TB Alliance and its partners, including the Novartis Institute for Tropical Diseases. In addition, three major pharmaceutical companies are devoting research facilities to the development of new drugs for TB: Novartis' Institute for Tropical Diseases in Singapore, AstraZeneca's facility in Bangalore, India, and GlaxoSmithKline's laboratories in Tres Cantos, Spain.

Box 4.6

Forecasting the potential benefits of a two-month drug regimen for tuberculosis

Current TB drugs impose a lengthy and complex regimen, which is widely recognized as a major challenge to TB control. In order to examine the benefits of new, faster acting drugs and their role in meeting the Millennium Development Goals targets, a team coordinated by the Global Alliance for TB Drug Development and overseen by the KNCV Tuberculosis Foundation developed an epidemiologic model of TB to forecast the impact of a shorter two-month regimen versus a standard six-month regimen in treatment programs.

The model is calibrated to different geographic regions. Regional analyses point to several general findings:

- Where cure rates are low, shortening therapy can have a major epidemiologic impact.
- Where case detection rates are low, shorter regimens may offer substantial benefits by enabling expansion of coverage.
- Even where DOTS targets are attained, new drugs can enhance outcomes.

Results are presented here for the example of the Southeast Asia region, as defined by the World Health Organization (including 5 of the 22 high-burden countries: India, Indonesia, Bangladesh, Thailand, and Myanmar).

The study considered various alternative baselines representing possible future treatment conditions in the absence of new, shorter regimens. In an example of a baseline scenario in which DOTS case-detection (of new smear-positive cases) in this region persists at the reported 2002 level of approximately 35 percent, three types of benefits are considered: reduced default through earlier treatment completion, reduced relapse after successful treatment, and enhanced case-detection made possible by reduced resource demands of a two-month versus six-month treatment regimen (figure 1). The study estimated the potential gains through 2030 if the new regimens were introduced starting in 2012. In this example, the total number of new cases between 2005 and 2030 could be reduced by 7–21 percent

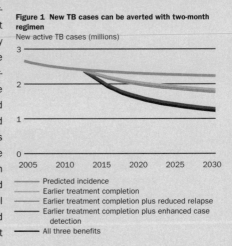

Figure 1 New TB cases can be averted with two-month regimen

New active TB cases (millions)

Predicted incidence
Earlier treatment completion
Earlier treatment completion plus reduced relapse
Earlier treatment completion plus enhanced case detection
All three benefits

A modeling study commissioned by the UN Millennium Project Working Group on TB looked into the potential benefits from developing drugs that could treat TB in two months rather than six months. The study suggests that new two-month therapies introduced within the decade have the potential not only to reverse the increasing disease incidence trend, but also to amplify the impact of DOTS, by the 2015 Millennium Development Goals target. If such new, faster acting drugs can be introduced by 2012, they could save up to 6 million lives and prevent nearly 13 million new cases of TB by 2030 (box 4.6).

New vaccines. A vaccine that strengthens the response to initial TB infection, or that boosts immunity in later life, could have an immense impact on disease

(4.7–12.8 million cases) under various combinations of these three types of benefits, and total deaths (not shown) could be reduced by 12–27 percent (2.6–5.9 million deaths).

To consider the implications of delays in developing new treatment technologies, the study team conducted both a retrospective analysis of the hypothetical gains that might have been realized with a new drug introduced in 2002, as well as a more pessimetical projection of the benefits missed by delaying introduction until 2022. The total number of averted cases through 2030 if the drug is introduced in 2012 could be as high as 12.8 million. If the shorter regimen had been available in 2002, an additional 12.1 million new cases might have been prevented (paler area in figure 2). Further delay could result in a missed opportunity to prevent 9.6 million cases (darker area in figure 2).

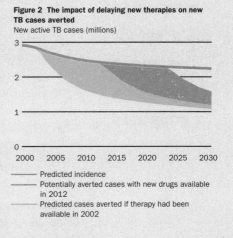

Figure 2 The impact of delaying new therapies on new TB cases averted

New active TB cases (millions)

Predicted incidence

Potentially averted cases with new drugs available in 2012

Predicted cases averted if therapy had been available in 2002

While additional analysis, particularly for regions with a high prevalence of HIV or high levels of MDR-TB, is ongoing, the findings here highlight the opportunities to make a substantial public health impact by introducing new technologies that could shorten TB treatment. The analysis shown in figure 1 demonstrates that new and improved therapies introduced within the decade can not only reverse the increasing disease incidence trend, but also amplify the impact of DOTS, by the 2015 Millennium Development Goals target.

Details of the study methodology are given in appendix 7.

Principal investigators: Dr. Joshua Salomon, Harvard School of Public Health, and Dr. Wayne Getz, University of California-Berkeley.

Other investigators: Megan Murray, Harvard University; Travis Porco, University of California, Berkeley; Steve Resch, Harvard University; Maria Sanchez, University of California, Berkeley; James Lloyd-Smith, University of California, Berkeley; and Milt Weinstein, Harvard University.

Advisors: Drs. Martien Borgdorff and Frank Cobelens, KNCV Tuberculosis Foundation.

control by preventing new cases and by reducing transmission. An effective vaccine may also be the best deterrent against the spread of MDR-TB.

Decoding of the genome sequence and development of genetic tools for *M. tuberculosis* have stimulated generation of a wide range of new vaccine candidates. More than 200 of these vaccine candidates have been tested in laboratory models of disease. The most promising candidates—those that are able to provide protection better than BCG—are now being advanced to clinical trials. The timeframe for vaccine development is determined in large part by the dynamics of the disease process: several years of monitoring will be required to evaluate whether or not disease develops in a vaccinated individual as part of Phase III efficacy trials. If the current generation of

Stop TB
partners
should work
to ensure that
new tools
respond to
the greatest
demand in
developing
countries

candidates performs well in clinical trials, a new vaccine could be available by 2012.

Recommendations

- Donor agencies should increase their investments in the research and development of new and affordable TB diagnostics, drugs, and vaccines through public-private partnerships, and in related projects such as the strengthening of clinical trials capacity in DOTS programs.
- The Stop TB Partnership and WHO should advocate for these investments to complement their access and treatment efforts. Advocacy should be based on a clear definition of the economic and social justifications of investing in new tools.
- Regulatory agencies should help harmonize streamlined regulatory requirements for introducing new TB diagnostics, drugs, and vaccines.
- The network of Stop TB partners should work to ensure that new tools respond to the greatest demands of users, and should expedite testing and roll-out in high-burden settings.

Operational research

Alongside the development of new tools, substantially more operational research is needed to determine the best ways to implement and monitor the impact of current interventions.

Operational research—"research aimed at developing interventions that result in improved policymaking, better design and implementation of health systems, and more efficient methods of service delivery" has a proud history in TB control (Nunn and others 2002). It was Karel Styblo's seminal work in Tanzania that led to the development of the DOTS strategy, as well as to a rise in cure rates from around 30 percent to over 80 percent in that pre-HIV era (Styblo and Chum 1987). The value and potential of operational research today is evident in operational research projects that have emerged from countries such as India and Malawi (Salaniponi and others 1999). In Malawi, many of the findings were translated into policy and practice because the research was undertaken within a disease control program and related directly to its problems (box 4.7).

Much of the information that emerges from operational research is currently made available through professional journals, national meetings, and international symposia. However, more needs to be done to make operational outcomes quickly available for use by the individuals organizing treatment programs in local settings. Given access to the Internet by NGOs and community associations, even in many low-income settings, there is an unprecedented opportunity for effective dissemination of practical information drawing on local experience.

A systematic and multilateral plan to increase the use of operational research relating to TB control should:

Box 4.7

Malawi national operational research program in tuberculosis

Source: Adapted from personal communication with Dr. Anthony Harries.

Malawi provides a very successful example of a national operational research program in TB. Health systems research in TB control began in Malawi in 1994 with the recognition that the National TB Control Program (NTP) was not coping with the dramatic increase in cases fueled by HIV: cases were diagnosed without adequate investigation, "hot spots" of transmission were suspected, and cure rates were poor.

The College of Medicine and the NTP set up research studies to address these problems with initial support from WHO. The diagnostic process and its shortcomings were analyzed in detail; different screening methods for diagnosis were explored; healthcare staff's adherence to NTP guidelines was assessed; the association between HIV and TB treatment outcome was defined; and the prevalence of TB in "hot spot" areas such as prisons and healthcare institutions was measured. A program management group that developed and implemented control and research strategy was formed.

Operational research became an integral component of the NTP and the research agenda was firmly linked to the objectives of its five-year development plan. During a seven-year period, over 100 research papers were published, many in international peer-reviewed journals. More importantly, however, because the research was undertaken within the structure of a disease control program and answered questions directly relevant to disease control, many of the findings were translated into policy and practice.

Two examples illustrate this practical response to research findings.

- One study showed that over 40 percent of smear-positive TB patients had spent at least one month with a traditional healer before coming to orthodox medical care. The NTP has since trained over 3,000 traditional healers in 15 districts.
- The incidence of TB in healthcare staff was found to be 3.6 percent per year. The NTP produced guidelines to reduce nosocomial TB transmission for use in every hospital.

This close integration of research with program activities has attracted further funds from a variety of donors.

- Ensure that sufficient, qualified operational researchers are available in low-income countries.
- Assess training needs systematically (such as the development of region-specific field-training manuals).
- Bridge the gulf between disease control personnel and academic researchers.
- Generate opportunities for operational researchers to interact, especially at the regional and country levels.
- Provide adequate funding.

Recommendation

- Operational research to determine the best ways to implement current interventions, and to monitor their impact, needs to be substantially increased. This requires financial and technical support for national TB programs to enhance local capacity for such research.

Recommendation 7: support the Global Plan to Stop TB

Generating widespread political commitment to effective TB control has been a key focus of activity over the last few years. The commitment of national governments, donor governments and agencies, UN agencies, and other bodies to the Stop TB Partnership and its Global Plan represents a reinforced political commitment to tackle TB.

Rationale

Explicit expressions of political commitment have been made by senior political leaders in a series of international gatherings. In 2000, ministerial representatives of 20 high-burden countries at the Amsterdam conference issued the Amsterdam Declaration to Stop TB, committing themselves to "ensuring that sufficient human and financial resources are available on a sustainable basis and expanded to meet the challenges of stopping TB." Similar statements were issued by African heads of state at the Abuja Summit in 2000, and—as the Washington Commitment to Stop TB—by partners at the first Stop TB Partners Forum in Washington in 2001.

Such public pronouncements yield their full value only when translated into practical action, maintained over time. National leaders have not always increased resources commensurate with their publicly stated international commitments (WHO 2004e), nor acted vigorously enough to secure sufficient political will to tackle only seriously at all levels within their own countries. Reports from the 22 high-burden countries in 2003 indicated that 8 saw wavering political commitment, either centrally or locally, as a continued obstruction to TB control efforts (WHO 2004j). In particular, countries with systems that were recently decentralized are finding it hard to expand DOTS because they lack local political support. Solutions include providing better support to local government following decentralization, forming provincial task forces, and building country-level advocacy for TB control. A coordinated and multifaceted effort to build political will, and to translate that commitment into effective public policy and programming, is an essential prerequisite to the expansion of DOTS programs.

Similar practical commitment to stop TB needs to be shown at the international level too. Regrettably, the UN Millennium Project does not specify TB alongside HIV/AIDS and malaria under Millennium Development Goal 6, despite overwhelming evidence of the scale of devastation wrought by the TB epidemic. Millennium Development Goal 6 should be amended to read: "Combat HIV/AIDS, malaria, tuberculosis, and other diseases."

What is needed and what is committed comes together in the Global Plan to Stop TB. The Global Plan provides the roadmap for achieving the Millennium Development Goal targets and sets the course for eventual elimination of TB as a public health problem. Long-term planning and sustainable financing are crucial to success. Work to extend the Global Plan to 2015 is already under way. It must support national planning, targeted for effective execution.

Recommendations

- All those involved at global, national, and local levels should come together to invest in the Global Plan to Stop TB, implement its key interventions, and work together to secure its targets: halving TB prevalence and deaths by 2015.
- Ministries of health in countries badly affected by TB should ensure dedicated budget lines for TB control activities. They should address TB control needs as part of poverty reduction strategies and efforts to strengthen health systems.

Chapter 5

Financing needs

The Stop TB Partnership is just beginning work on a comprehensive Global Plan to Stop TB II (2006–2015). Updated figures for the resources needed to achieve the target for tuberculosis (TB) in line with the recommendations of this report will be provided as part of developing this Global Plan. Having an integrated plan and budget is critical to guide donors and the global TB community on overall financing needs to control TB worldwide.

Why more resources are needed

The 2004 "Progress Report on the First Global Plan to Stop TB" estimates an annual resource gap between what is needed and what is available of at least $1 billion for global TB control and new tool development (Stop TB Partnership/WHO 2004c). These estimates were made with reference to a particular set of control targets to cover the basic essential needs. However, this report of the UN Millennium Project Working Group on TB advocates that countries adopt comprehensive TB control with mainstreamed TB/HIV and DOTS-Plus interventions. This means that the cost of TB control cannot avoid increasing, and the $1 billion gap will underestimate resource requirements.

For DOTS expansion, cost estimates in the 2004 progress report focused on reaching the global target of detecting 70 percent of sputum smear–positive cases and successfully treating 85 percent of those detected. Although the estimates included treatment for new smear-negative and extrapulmonary cases as well, they do not allow for the costs of detecting and treating all cases.

For TB/HIV collaborative activities, earlier cost estimates were initially limited to just 12 countries and were made prior to greatly expanded plans to scale up AIDS testing and treatment, notably delivery of antiretroviral treatment. Recent provisional estimates for an expanded set of TB/HIV collabora-

The Global Drug Facility has been remarkably effective

tive activities suggest that costs will be at least double those projected in the original Global Plan, largely because of including antiretroviral treatment.[1]

In addition, significantly increased resources will be needed in the future to address the growing epidemic of MDR-TB, particularly as better methods to detect people with MDR-TB become available. Current estimates in the Global Plan Progress Report would cover just 10 percent of MDR-TB patients. The cost of drugs remains high. Even drugs obtained through the Green Light Committee cost up to $1,000 per treatment, and without committee approval, the cost can be $10,000–$15,000.

TB high-burden countries, particularly the wealthier developing countries, currently shoulder most of the costs for DOTS expansion through national budgetary allocations or borrowings from the World Bank. A number of these countries have the capacity to provide additional resources to expand TB efforts. Funds allocated in the national budgets of high-burden countries for TB control programs are important indicators of political commitment.

Poorer high-burden nations are more likely to need external funding to supply a larger proportion of their national TB control efforts, especially as DOTS efforts are scaled up. In addition, the original Global Plan to Stop TB found that only a small portion of the costs for scaling up TB/HIV activities and treating MDR-TB were borne by national governments. Increased donor support is vital for expanding scale-up efforts and for accelerating new tool development.

About the critical issue of drug supply, the Global Drug Facility (GDF) has been shown by evaluations to be a remarkably effective mechanism for providing countries with supplies of high-quality, low-cost first-line drugs. Yet, despite its success in filling the drug gap, the GDF is facing a funding shortfall in 2004 and 2005. Overall, annual GDF spending was $20.4 million cumulatively for its first two years of operation (2001 and 2002) and $15.6 million in 2003. For 2004, the GDF projects a need of $29.7 million and $43.2 million in 2005 just to meet existing commitments and support its operation. Of the projected needs for 2004 and 2005, the GDF is facing a funding gap of $13.6 million in 2004 and $26.2 million in 2005. Ideally, the GDF needs $50 million annually to approve new applications and award additional grants to countries in need.

The Green Light Committee, which addresses the gap for second-line drugs to treat MDR-TB using the DOTS-Plus strategy, has so far provided treatment to 4,500 multidrug-resistant patients, yet this covers less than 2 percent of the annual number of new MDR-TB cases estimated worldwide. Without greater priority to support the Green Light Committee and DOTS-Plus programs, the burden of MDR-TB will remain large and treatment will be much more expensive than necessary.

Research and development

The costs of research and development of new tools for 2004 and 2005 are estimated to be around $210 million per year, compared with estimated TB treatment costs of almost $4 billion worldwide annually. The R&D costs cover a broad range of activities, from basic research to registration, undertaken by a wide array of institutions. The majority of the costs is expected to be borne by the private-public partnerships (FIND, TB Alliance, and AREAS) as they take the lead in developing a core portfolio and catalyzing the global pipeline of diagnostics, drugs, and vaccines.

New diagnostics

The Global Plan to Stop TB 2001–2005 estimated a need of roughly $150 million in R&D costs over five years to develop new diagnostic tools. Costs for 2004 and 2005 are estimated at around $30 million per year.

New drug development

The Global Plan to Stop TB estimated the costs of drug development activities over five years to be close to $350 million, as the first phase of an undertaking projected to last at least a decade. The total current funding gap is $112 million for 2004 and 2005.

Turberculosis vaccine development

The Global Plan to Stop TB projected $420 million over five years in TB vaccine R&D costs. Costs for 2004 and 2005 are roughly estimated at $100 million per year. These costs include approximately $40 million each year to maintain current levels of preclinical research and a similar amount to maintain Phase I and II trials for five candidate vaccines. The remaining $20 million per year is required to build capacity for Phase III trials for successful vaccine candidates.

Annual external aid for TB control in developing countries stood at $210 million in 2002 (an increase from $16 million in 1990 and $40–$50 million in 1995). Substantial new funding has become available since mid-2002, principally from increased investments from the Global Fund to Fight AIDS, Tuberculosis, and Malaria and from donors—including new World Bank loans for China and Russia, and greatly increased support for TB control from the United States Agency for International Development, the Canadian International Development Agency, and the U.K. Department for International Development. Additional resources from donors will be essential in order to fill the funding gap for treatment, especially in poorer countries, and for R&D.

Since its inception in 2001, the GFATM has made substantial funding contributions to TB control. By the end of 2003, the fund had approved a total five-year budget of $608 million for TB proposals, and a further $319 million for combined TB/HIV proposals. The projected outcomes from GFATM-approved programs over five years are an additional 3.5 million TB cases being treated under DOTS and 12,000 new DOTS-Plus treatments for MDR-TB.

**The costs
of drug
development
activities over
five years
are close to
$350 million**

High-burden TB countries are the main beneficiaries; only three (Brazil, Nigeria, and Zimbabwe) have not received GFATM awards.[2]

The GFATM is a critically important new funder of TB control. However, although GFATM funding has filled some shortfalls in national TB program finances, it has still not increased commensurate with need and opportunity, and it is still an underused resource. Furthermore, the GFATM is itself facing severe resource constraints because of underfunding by external donors and may be unable to award new grants in 2005 and beyond.

On the implementation side, the case study on achieving the TB target in Kenya undertaken for this report found that disbursement of funds by the GFATM has been slow. From Kenya's first two-year grant of $4.9 million, to date only an initial disbursement of $839,416, in August 2003, has been made. Similar delays have been experienced in other countries, such as Bangladesh, Indonesia, and Myanmar. This has important consequences, as delays in disbursement are likely to hinder the implementation of proposed activities needed to reverse the trend in TB incidence.

Estimate of general health system requirements

More generally, the 2001 Commission on Macroeconomics and Health estimated global funding needs for general health infrastructure and the necessary improvements to provide the essential package of care with full population access (CMH 2001). The estimated additional annual financing needed to deliver the essential package of care in 83 poor countries is $57 billion in 2007 and $94 billion in 2015. This includes both the costs of disease-specific activities and the costs of strengthening health systems to deliver these at scale. Clearly, achieving global targets for health, including TB targets, requires investment in the general health infrastructure as well as in disease-specific activities. Those concerned with TB control must join forces with those concerned with delivering the overall essential package of care to demand the necessary investments in general health infrastructure improvements.

Recommendations

- The UN Millennium Project Working Group on TB endorses the recommendation of the WHO Executive Board to the 2005 World Health Assembly, encouraging all countries to fulfill their commitment to ensure the availability of sufficient domestic resources and of sufficient external resources to achieve the 2015 Millennium Development Goals target relevant to TB.
- Updated figures for the resources required to achieve the target in line with the recommendations of this report should be provided as part of developing the Global Plan to Stop TB II, 2006–2015. These estimates should be used to advocate for increased levels of funding for TB con-

trol and new tools research and development that are commensurate with the global burden of TB and will provide the full resources needed to reverse this epidemic.

- Adequate GFATM funding and increased GFATM support for TB and TB/HIV efforts need to be ensured.
- Technical support is needed to develop and implement GFATM-financed projects and programs supported by other sources of finance.
- Additional investment for the private-public research partnerships should be catalyzed, including investment from national governments and other sources.
- It will be important to ensure that funding for TB control becomes more predictable and that any new financing mechanisms, such as the GFATM, are truly additional to existing resources.

Chapter 6

Meeting the target in UN Millennium Project pilot countries

One core task of the UN Millennium Project is working with several countries to identify the specific, integrated public policy interventions and investments required to enable the countries to meet the Millennium Development Goals by 2015. Working with the relevant UN Country Teams, the UN Millennium Project is assisting governments to develop Goals-based, three- to five-year poverty reduction strategies (including Poverty Reduction Strategy Papers) in the context of 2015 planning horizons.

UN Millennium Project pilot country case studies

The UN Millennium Project is working in a number of countries where the government is committed to the Millennium Development Goals: Bangladesh, Cambodia, the Dominican Republic, Ethiopia, Ghana, Kenya, Senegal, Tajikistan, and Yemen. Of these, Cambodia, Ethiopia, and Kenya are high-burden tuberculosis (TB) countries.

The Working Group on TB has undertaken a set of four country case studies that review the progress each country has made to date toward the achievement of the TB-related Millennium Development Goals target, assess remaining gaps, and discuss necessary future steps. A detailed study has been undertaken for Kenya because it is a TB high-burden country, is representative of many Sub-Saharan African countries with concomitant high levels of TB and HIV, and has a well-established and effective national TB control program (appendix 2). Briefer studies are provided for three other countries: Cambodia (appendix 3), the Dominican Republic (appendix 4), and Ethiopia (appendix 5). Key findings are summarized below; the full reports can be found in the appendixes.

No field research or new analyses were conducted for these studies; they draw on a wide array of existing documents, including country TB program

The funding gap for TB control activities must be closed

material and Global Fund Applications, and WHO, World Bank, and other UN databases. The goal for these analyses has been to provide a brief country overview and to draw from multiple sources to begin to discuss how best the countries can meet the target of reversing the incidence of TB by 2015.

Meeting the tuberculosis target in Kenya

Kenya's basic health indices have worsened over the past decade, indicating the continued deterioration of the population's health status and quality of life. The country's total expenditure on health has not changed much over the past five years, with roughly 4 percent of total health spending being devoted to TB control. Total health expenditure per capita was $29 in 2001 with only $6 coming from the government. Poverty levels in Kenya are also evidence of the deteriorating economic situation. In addition, the HIV/AIDS epidemic has had devastating economic effects for the country.

In 2004, Kenya ranked 12th among the 22 high-burden TB countries. The total number of TB cases reported to the National Leprosy and TB Control Program in 2003 was 95,310, a sevenfold increase since 1990. Case notification rates for sputum smear–positive pulmonary TB cases have been rising over the past decade. Currently, WHO estimates that 51 percent of adult TB cases in Kenya are among people infected with HIV.

Although Kenya's treatment success rate of 80 percent is close to the 85 percent target, the 49 percent case detection rate of new sputum smear–positive cases is far from the 70 percent target. Identifying those "missing cases" and improving surveillance to determine the actual outcomes of all cases must be addressed for Kenya to achieve the Millennium Development Goals target.

Challenges

Kenya has formidable challenges in its path to reversing the rising trend of TB incidence. Its health system is suffering tremendously under the burden of chronic inadequate resources and from the toll taken by the HIV/AIDS epidemic.

There is a shortage of both financial and human resources available to combat TB in Kenya. Although external funds will help decrease the gap over the next five years, a shortfall of finances will remain. The health expenditure per capita for Kenya is well below the estimated level necessary for providing essential services.

TB/HIV modeling data suggest that if the current course is continued in Kenya, TB incidence will continue to rise. Projections indicate that the incidence of TB in Kenya can be halted or reversed only if HIV prevalence decreases.

In Kenya, there is a significant association between TB case detection rates and the prevalence of poverty in a province, with the poorest provinces reporting the most cases. However, recent studies have suggested that the poor are under-

Joint activities between TB and HIV/ AIDS control programs must be stepped up

represented in the health system overall and in TB services specifically. This combination suggests that many of the "missing" cases are among the poor.

A significant proportion of TB patients in Kenya receive care from the private sector, which provides approximately half of all health services. TB patients diagnosed and treated in the private sector are frequently not reported to the National Leprosy and TB Control Program and, therefore, are not included in annual morbidity and mortality data or reports of treatment outcomes.

Since DOTS relies on passive case finding, general knowledge among the population about common TB symptoms and where to seek care is essential. Data from Kenya has shown a lack of community knowledge about TB symptoms, TB transmission, and the potential for cure in the presence of HIV co-infection. A study in 2000 noted lengthy diagnostic delays as patients often tried multiple home remedies, nonprescription medicines, and herbal or traditional therapies before presenting for medical care. Stigma was also reported to exist within families, among healthcare providers, and in the community. Few patients with TB symptoms who had accessed care knew that TB treatment was available free of charge through the public sector.

Recommendations

Kenya has achieved great progress in its TB control efforts over the past decade: the DOTS strategy has been accepted as national TB control policy and implemented countrywide, and treatment success rate is close to the 2005 target of 85 percent. Case detection, at 49 percent, is well above the global average of 37 percent. However, if Kenya remains on its current course of TB control activities, it will not reach the Millennium Development Goals target of halting and reversing TB incidence by 2015. The extraordinary challenges Kenya is facing require extraordinary action.

- Human resources development is critically needed. The prime requirement of strengthening the human capacity at all National Leprosy and TB Control Program levels must be complemented by more targeted training and improved staff development to allow better use of existing human resources.
- The funding gap for TB control activities must be closed. Government health expenditures per capita should be increased from $6 to $35–$40, a range that will cover scaling up the activities necessary for achieving the Millennium Development Goals target for TB.
- Joint activities between TB and HIV/AIDS control programs must be stepped up. In addition to plans for intensified case finding, improved case holding, and treatment of latent TB among HIV-infected individuals, the introduction of antiretrovirals on a broad scale is needed. This will require greatly increased access to HIV testing and counseling for TB patients. Widespread antiretroviral use has been predicted to prevent about 50 percent of active TB cases.

Many of the recommended activities are overlapping and inter-dependent

- TB control programming must include interventions to target the poor. Directed interventions are needed to improve access to care in the public sector by removing hidden costs, raising awareness of TB symptoms and appropriate care options, and offering community-based options.
- A national communication strategy is needed to address the issues of stigma and lack of knowledge about TB and care options, and, once it is diagnosed, to improve adherence to treatment.
- To rapidly scale up DOTS delivery by private sector providers, DOTS must be promoted as the standard of care through existing private association and academic forums. Private sector involvement in TB care can improve access, link TB care with HIV care, develop human resources, target the poor, and close the private provider reporting loophole. It thus addresses multiple constraints simultaneously.

The constraints and recommended strategies have been outlined to indicate the path forward. Many of the recommended activities are overlapping and interdependent. For example, human resources development is necessary for essentially every proposed activity, and mobilizing the private sector will help target services to the poor. Significant resources will be needed if Kenya is to set the example for other high-burden TB countries (particularly high-burden TB/HIV countries) and reach the Millennium Development Goals target by 2015.

This analysis of meeting the TB target in Kenya has been reviewed by the Kenya National Leprosy and TB Control Program to ensure that it accurately reflects the constraints, priorities, and current direction of the program.

Meeting the tuberculosis target in other UN Millennium Project pilot countries: Cambodia, the Dominican Republic, and Ethiopia

A quick profile of the current TB and HIV status for other UN Millennium Project pilot countries shows the significant association of these diseases with poverty and public health spending (table 6.1). Figures reflect the most recent data available for each country from World Development Indicators, WHO, and UNAIDS.

The three brief country case studies included in appendixes to this report were chosen from three distinct regions of the world. Each of these countries has unique cultural traditions, social institutional systems, regional influences, and political and historical trajectories. There are also significant commonalities, many of which are the consequences of a large number of people living in poverty. Vulnerability to both chronic health problems and a wide array of serious infectious diseases including TB stems from the negative impact of poverty on every feature of life including housing, water and sanitation systems, quality and quantity of reliable food supplies, quality and accessibility of educational institutions, and access to both primary and specialized health services.

Table 6.1
Tuberculosis and poverty

Note: SS+ is sputum smear–positive.

Source: WHO 2004j.

Country	SS+ TB prevalence per 100,000 population	SS+ TB incidence per 100,000 population	TB incidence, all cases per 100,000 population	TB mortality per 100,000 population	DOTS population coverage (percent)	Percent adult TB cases that are also HIV+	Percent population reported below poverty line	Public health expenditure (percent of GDP)
Bangladesh	188	99	221	52	95	0.1	50	1.5
Cambodia	311	242	549	107	100	14	36	1.7
Dominican Republic	56	42	95	18	40	13	29	2.2
Ethiopia	265	159	370	88	95	29	44	1.1
Ghana	156	93	211	51	100	16	40	2.8
Kenya	296	223	540	132	100	51	52	1.7
Senegal	170	108	242	108	100	2.9	NA	2.8
Tajikistan	79	49	109	19	13	0	NA	0.9

**What is
needed now
is expansion,
adaptation,
and
investment of
demonstrably
successful
approaches**

Of these three countries, two—Ethiopia and Cambodia—are classified by the World Bank as low-income countries; the Dominican Republic is classified as a low-middle income country. All three countries are indebted to varying degrees, but only Ethiopia has qualified for debt relief. All three have a significant number of their populations below, or near, the poverty line.

Both Ethiopia and Cambodia are among the 22 countries with a high burden of TB. The Dominican Republic has lower incidences of TB relative to the other two countries, but it carries a higher burden of drug-resistant TB. Not coincidentally, all three countries also carry significant burdens of HIV infection. While Cambodia has had decreased HIV prevalence over the last two years, both the Dominican Republic and Ethiopia continue to see increasing prevalence.

Addressing the TB epidemic in an individual country must necessarily reflect societal structures, local culture, and the characteristics of existing health and governance systems that comprise the country-specific context. However, because many of the constraints encountered relate both to the burden of poverty shared to varying degrees by these countries and to the HIV pandemic, there are some common themes in recommendations made to assist countries in halting and reversing the incidence of TB:

- Include the economic and social burden of the TB epidemic, as well as a detailed plan of action to address it, as part of all poverty reduction strategies developed within the countries.
- Address and remove barriers of access to health services in general and TB treatment in particular. These barriers include economic obstacles for poor people. In all three of these countries (but especially in Ethiopia and Cambodia), geographic issues of rural distance and isolation from services and affordable transportation to services must be addressed.
- Increase health spending per capita.
- Strengthen collaborative relationships between TB and HIV units at all levels of the health system.
- Develop community-based services tailored to the needs and characteristics of communities.
- Promote program-based operational research, including an appraisal of the local barriers to TB services and proposed interventions to overcome them. Develop and document country-specific best practices.

Conclusion

I am living proof that TB can be beaten. With treatment, TB patients can be cured; TB untreated is life-threatening. Share the responsibility and share the reward of knowing you are saving lives. Every breath does count, so stop TB now and let people live!

—Archbishop Desmond Tutu, Nobel Laureate
(2nd Stop TB Partners' Forum, March 2004)

Box 6.1	Problem	Key interventions	Focus and level of interventions

Recommended key interventions to meet the Millennium Development Goals target for tuberculosis	TB: 2 million deaths and 9 million new cases per year.	To ensure access for all to high quality TB care:
		• Implement the DOTS strategy:
		  1. Political commitment.
		  2. Diagnosis with sputum smear microscopy.
		  3. Standardized short-course chemotherapy.
		  4. Consistent supply of essential TB drugs.
		  5. Standardized recording and reporting systems.
		• Implement collaborative interventions against TB and against HIV, to control HIV-related TB.
		• Mainstream DOTS-Plus adaptation in high MDR-TB settings.
		• Accelerate development and use of new tools for diagnosis, treatment, and prevention.
			The full range of providers in the public and private sectors and the community should deliver the international standard of care, in line with the DOTS strategy.
			• Community partnership and outreach, grassroots mobilization.
			• Strategic focus on
			  1. 22 TB high-burden countries, which account for 80 percent of all TB cases.
			  2. Sub-Saharan Africa, because of poverty and HIV-related TB.
			  3. Poor people.
			• Public-private partnerships for developing new tools, and local engagement for testing new diagnostics, drugs, and vaccines.

The target to halve the prevalence of TB disease and deaths by 2015 is certainly achievable. The basic pillars of a successful plan are understood and widely accepted. They include structures, strategies, and supplies.

What is needed now is expansion, adaptation, and investment of demonstrably successful approaches based on DOTS. In many cases, the necessary instruments are already in place, though tackling TB/HIV effectively demands more far-reaching changes in approaches and attitudes. Also critical are the mainstreaming of DOTS-Plus into DOTS programs and intensified support for creating new drugs, diagnostics, and vaccines.

Key interventions recommended in this report are summarized in box 6.1. A full list of recommendations is given in appendix 8. These recommendations must be accompanied by a broader initiative to strengthen depleted health systems. Success will require political commitment and effective advocacy and communications. Backed by sufficient and sustained support nationally and internationally over the next 10 years, these measures provide the blueprint for turning the tide of TB by 2015.

World Health Organization recommendations for implementing the DOTS strategy and its adaptations

The development of new tools for tuberculosis (TB) control (such as a more effective vaccine, better diagnostic tests, and improved preventive and therapeutic approaches) holds out the prospect of rapid progress in TB control in the future. In the meantime, maximizing the impact of currently available methods of diagnosis and treatment entails implementing the DOTS strategy and its adaptations as effectively and as widely as possible. This appendix summarizes the key features of the DOTS strategy and three of the main adaptations to it:

- The expanded strategy to control HIV-related TB.
- DOTS-Plus to control multidrug-resistant tuberculosis (MDR-TB).
- Public-private mix DOTS to engage private practitioners in TB control.

The DOTS strategy
In coordination with a global network of partners known as the DOTS Expansion Working Group, WHO is committed to implementing the DOTS strategy as effectively and as widely as possible (WHO 2002c).

WHO published the "Global DOTS Expansion Plan" in 2001 (WHO 2001b). The plan is based on two pillars:

- The preparation in each country of a medium-term (at least five years) DOTS expansion plan.
- The establishment of a mechanism for interagency coordination ensuring that all relevant partners contribute to the implementation of the national plan.

Effective development and implementation of the national plan depend on the engagement of the full range of health providers under national TB programs stewardship: government services, whether ministry of health (nationally and locally administrated services) or not (examples are social security schemes, prisons, and the military), and nongovernment services, such as those provided by NGOs, community groups, private practitioners, and employers (WHO 2003b, 2003c; Lönnroth and others 2004). In practice, all health providers should either refer patients to public health facilities delivering TB care under the DOTS strategy or deliver TB care consistent with the DOTS strategy in collaboration with the national TB program. The failure of providers to deliver care consistent with the DOTS strategy as the internationally recommended standard compromises the achievements of national TB programs and the chances of successful TB control. Governments should consider reforming legislative and regulatory frameworks to engage the full range of health providers. They will need to invest in developing human resource capacity for strengthened national TB program stewardship and service delivery (WHO 2001a).

The expanded strategy to control HIV-related tuberculosis

Until recently, efforts to control TB among HIV-infected people have mainly focused on identifying and curing infectious TB cases among patients presenting to general health services. This targets the final step in the sequence of events by which HIV fuels TB—the transmission of *M. tuberculosis* infection by infectious TB cases.

The expanded strategy for TB control in high HIV prevalence populations includes not only interventions against TB (the DOTS strategy and TB preventive treatment) but also interventions against HIV (and therefore indirectly against TB), such as providing and teaching about condoms, treating sexually transmitted infections, safe injecting drug use, and using highly active antiretroviral treatment.

DOTS-Plus

DOTS-Plus refers to the programmatic approach to the diagnosis and treatment of MDR-TB within the context of DOTS programs. Management involves the diagnosis of MDR-TB through quality-assured culture and drug susceptibility testing and treatment with second-line drugs under proper case management conditions.

In response to the seriousness of MDR-TB as a global public health problem, the DOTS-Plus Working Group, one of seven working groups within the Stop TB Partnership was established in 1999 to promote improved management of MDR-TB in resource-limited countries. The DOTS-Plus Working Group aims to assess the feasibility and cost-effectiveness of the use of second-line drugs in DOTS-Plus projects. Since 2000, the Green Light Committee has successfully negotiated with the pharmaceutical industry substantial concessionary prices for second-line drugs that otherwise were unaffordable in poor settings. As a result, prices of the most expensive regimens have dropped by 95 percent.

The requirements for establishing DOTS-Plus projects include the following:

- Analyzing factors leading to the emergence of MDR-TB and implementing measures to address these factors.
- Defining project setting.
- Obtaining commitment from local and national health authorities to ensure project monitoring and evaluation in collaboration with the Green Light Committee.
- Mobilizing adequate resources for the duration of the project.
- Developing a detailed project manual with a work plan stating the commitment, responsibilities, and contributions of all stakeholders.
- Cooperating among agencies on technical aspects of the project.
- Formally endorsing project by national authorities.
- Planning for long-term sustainability of the project (including building local capacity to implement and evaluate the project).

Public-private mix DOTS

Public-private mix DOTS refers to the means of engaging private practitioners in collaboration with national TB programs in the delivery of TB care consistent with the DOTS strategy. This is necessary where large numbers of people who may be infected with TB seek care from private practitioners rather than from public health services. Recent studies indicate the success of the public-private mix approach in achieving high rates of case detection, notification, and cure (Lönnroth and others 2004).

A global subgroup of the DOTS-Expansion Working Group concerned with public-private mix DOTS is promoting the scaling up of this approach, accompanied by the necessary strengthening of the national TB program stewardship and leadership roles. Lessons learned from public-private mix DOTS are applicable to engaging the contributions of a wide range of public providers who in many countries are providing TB care independently of the national TB program, such as those in prisons and social security schemes.

The success factors for public-private mix DOTS include the following:

- Obtaining government commitment to national TB program stewardship functions.
- Financing public-private mix operations (including drug costs and cost for staff for supervision) and monitoring and evaluation activities.
- Involving public sector providers and requiring coordination on government levels and collaboration between different ministries
- Fostering dialogue among all stakeholders to build trust.
- Using an NGO or a medical association as a "neutral ground" to facilitate dialogue and collaboration.
- Training national TB program staff and private providers, and improving referral and information systems.

- Providing drugs free of charge to patients.

Following the demonstration of the feasibility and effectiveness of the public-private mix approach in pilot projects, the main challenge is to scale up the approach so that all patients receive TB care from private practitioners in line with the DOTS strategy.

Meeting the Millennium Development Goals target in Kenya

This in-depth case study outlines what is required for Kenya to achieve the Millennium Development Goals target for tuberculosis (TB) by 2015. Kenya was selected because it represents many Sub-Saharan African countries with concomitant high TB and HIV/AIDS burdens and has a well established and effective national TB control program. This case study describes the progress that Kenya has made achieving the target for TB, assesses remaining gaps and constraints, and makes recommendations about future necessary steps. Existing demographic and epidemiologic data and projections, health system assessments, relevant strategy and policy documents, and new health and poverty reduction initiatives were reviewed. No field research or new analyses were conducted in conjunction with the preparation of this study. The Kenya National Leprosy and TB Control Program (NLTP) provided its annual report, financial and epidemiological data, and other program-related information and reviewed this document to ensure that it accurately reflects the constraints, priorities, and current direction of the program.

Overview of Kenya's demographics

Of Kenya's 31,549,000 inhabitants, 42 percent are younger than age 15 and 3 percent are age 60 or older (UN 2002). The population growth rate is 1.96 percent with a birth rate of 34.5 per 1,000 (World Bank 2004). Life expectancy has dropped from 56.8 years in 1992 (prior to the full catastrophic impact of HIV/AIDS) to 45.5 years in 2002 (World Bank 2004). In 2002, 65 percent of the population was living in rural areas. Kenya's 2003 Demographic and Health Survey reported the infant and under-five mortality rates as 78 per 1,000 live births and 114 per 1,000 respectively (Kenya 2003); since 1989, both rates have increased by 30 percent. These and other worsening health indices indicate the continued deterioration of the Kenyan population's health status and quality of life.

After a period of moderately high growth in the 1960s and 1970s, Kenya's economy began to decline. In 2001, Kenya ranked 146 of 175 countries in the human development index and its Gini index was 44.5, meaning poor overall socioeconomic status of the population with inequalities in the distribution of income (UNDP 2003).[1] Its estimated gross domestic product (GDP) for 2002 was $12.3 billion with a GDP per capita of $1,020 (World Bank 2004). Unemployment remains high, particularly in urban areas; in 2002 an estimated 15 percent of the labor force was without a job, and in urban areas, the rate was reported to be 25 percent (Kenya 2002). Underemployment is also likely to be common. Poverty levels in Kenya are evidence of the deteriorating economic situation. In 2001, the prevalence of poverty at the national level was 56 percent, meaning that 56 percent of the population did not achieve the minimum income to obtain basic food and nonfood items.

The HIV/AIDS epidemic in Kenya has had devastating economic effects. Like TB, HIV/AIDS strikes people in their most productive years for income generation and family caretaking. The HIV/AIDS epidemic has been shown to decrease GDP in some countries, and may exacerbate income disparities and increase poverty overall.

Health services in Kenya

In 2001, the total expenditure on health (expressed as percent of GDP) was 7.8, which is essentially unchanged over the past five years (World Bank 2004). The majority of health expenditures was on private services (NLTP 2003a). Total (public and private) health expenditure per capita was $29 in 2001 (NLTP 2003a), a figure that had remained fairly constant during the preceding five-year period. In 2002, the countrywide total of medical personnel was 59,049, which included 4,740 physicians, 9,753 registered nurses, 29,094 enrolled nurses, and 4,778 clinical officers (Kenya 2002). These figures yield rates of 0.15 physicians per 1,000 population and 0.33 registered nurses per 1,000 population.

Launched in 1980, the NLTP is part of the Ministry of Health's Department of Preventive and Promotive Health Services and falls under the Division of AIDS/STI/TB/Leprosy. NLTP activities and services are delivered through 1,262 government health units, 227 NGO health units, and 73 private facilities as well as 810 laboratories, of which 619 are smear microscopy centers (NLTP 2003a). The NLTP is implementing activities according to its Development Plan 2001–2005; the action plan for 2005–2009 is being developed. Since 1996, DOTS coverage has been countrywide and all TB treatment is provided free of charge. The Ministry of Health is committed to procuring the bulk of anti-TB drugs with plans for the Global Drug Facility to fill any gaps. No drug stockouts were reported in 2003. The recently renovated central reference laboratory has capabilities for mycobacterial culture and drug susceptibility testing. In addition, four private labs in Nairobi with these capabilities are being networked with the central reference laboratory.

The NLTP is organized into three levels: national, provincial, and district. At the national level, a small core staff supports a cohesive national program. The TB program manager, appointed last year, is supported by a physician seconded from the Centers for Disease Control and Prevention and another medical officer. The staff also includes a coordinator for information, education and communication and advocacy activities, a health information technologist, a laboratory technician, and clinical officers for community TB care for hard-to-reach areas and remote populations. The provincial and district TB/leprosy coordinators are responsible for coordinating and supervising NLTP activities at their respective levels. TB control activities are integrated at the district level with other basic health services. The government of Kenya's National Health Sector Strategic Plan for 1999 to 2004 has guided health sector reform and the decentralization of health services.

The Kenyan NLTP is one of the few TB programs in the world that is administratively linked to the HIV/AIDS program. There is a joint plan to improve TB/HIV collaborative activities, including referring TB cases for HIV counseling and testing, screening HIV-infected individuals for active TB, and providing isoniazid prophylaxis to HIV-infected individuals in settings where compliance can be guaranteed (such as prisons). The NLTP anticipates hiring a coordinator of TB/HIV activities to ensure more substantial progress in the future.

Nearly 4 percent of the government's total health spending is for TB control activities (WHO 2004). The total public sector costs of TB control in Kenya for 2003 (including NLTP budgeted and nonbudgeted activities) were estimated to be $13.8 million (table A2.1). The 2003 total NLTP budget increased from the previous year to cover costs associated with DOTS expansion activities, increased staff for TB and TB/HIV, and drug costs for the anticipated increase in case detection. A funding gap was estimated at $3.3 million.

In 2003, Kenya received a $4.9 million award from the Global Fund to Fight AIDS, Tuberculosis, and Malaria (GFATM). These funds will support the NLTP's five-year plan to increase the coverage and quality of DOTS. The first award disbursement of $839,416 occurred in August 2003 (GFATM 2004b). Several international partners also contribute support, directly or indirectly, to TB control activities in Kenya.[2]

Tuberculosis epidemiology

Kenya ranked 12 among the 22 high-burden TB countries based on 2002 case notifications.[3] The number of TB cases reported to the NLTP in 2003 was 95,310, which represented an eightfold increase from the 11,788 cases reported in 1990. The number of sputum smear–positive pulmonary TB cases in 2003

Table A2.1	Required funding	Expected funding				Funding gap
		Government	Loans	Grants	Other	
National TB Program budget estimates, existing funding, and budget gaps in Kenya, fiscal year 2003	*National TB Program budget*					
($ millions)	Drugs	2.2	1.3	0.5	0.4	0	0
— *not available*	Dedicated TB control staff	5.1	1.0	0	0.4	0.4	3.3
a. WHO estimates; data not provided by the National TB Program. b. Estimates differ from those in Global TB Control 2003 due to a change in methods made possible by the availability of new data. See methods for full details.	New activities to raise case detection and cure rates	2.5	0	0	2.5	0	0
	Buildings, equipment, vehicles	—	—	0	—	0	0
	Other line items	1.2	1.2	0	0	0	0
Source: WHO 2004j.	Total	11.0	3.5	0.5	3.3	0.4	3.3
	Costs not covered by budget [a]					
	Hospital stay	0.5	0.5	0	0	0	0
	Clinic visits for DOT and monitoring	2.3	2.3	0	0	0	0
	Total costs not covered	2.8	2.8	0	0	0	0
	Total TB control costs	13.8	6.3	0.5	3.3	0.4	3.3

was 38,158, which is nearly 4,000 cases higher than the previous year. Case notification rates in 2003 were 295 per 100,000 population for all TB cases and 118 per 100,000 population for sputum smear–positive pulmonary TB cases; these rates have quadrupled and tripled respectively over the past decade.

The majority of TB cases reported in 2003 were new smear-positive pulmonary cases (42 percent). Compared with the previous year, there was a slight decrease in the proportion of new smear-positive cases and a slight increase in the proportion of re-treatment cases. Despite recent reports of increasing rates of drug resistance in Kenya, consistently low treatment failure rates (0.4 percent among both new smear-positive and re-treatment cases registered in 2002) suggest that MDR-TB rates in Kenya are low. Data from a 2002 national survey of drug resistance should soon be available.

There is little country-specific data from Kenya documenting the impact of the HIV/AIDS epidemic on TB rates. A 1994 national survey of TB patients showed the HIV sera-prevalence rate among TB patients to be approximately 41 percent. Currently, WHO estimates that 51 percent of adult TB cases are among people infected with HIV (WHO 2004j). Results of HIV testing from Kenya's 2003 Demographic and Health Survey found 6.7 percent of the respondents tested to be HIV positive. HIV prevalence was higher among women (9 percent compared with 5 percent of men tested) and among those tested in urban areas (10 percent compared with 6 percent in rural areas). The province with the highest percentage of HIV-positive respondents was Nyanza (14 percent) followed by Nairobi (9 percent); these are the provinces with the largest numbers of TB cases and among those with the greatest annual increase.

Treatment success among new smear-positive pulmonary TB cases from the 2002 cohort was 80 percent (65 percent cured). This rate has been fairly constant since the implementation of DOTS. High treatment interruption and transferred out rates (9 percent and 7 percent respectively) suggest that many of these cases may actually represent underreported deaths. Kenya's case detection rate of new smear-positive cases is low at 49 percent. Identifying those "missing cases" and improving surveillance to determine the actual outcomes of cases closed as transferred out must be addressed for Kenya to achieve the TB target.

Challenges to achieving the target

Kenya has several formidable challenges in its path to reversing the rising trend of TB incidence. Kenya's health system is suffering tremendously under the burden of chronic inadequate resources and from the toll taken by the HIV/AIDS epidemic. This is the context—that of an ailing health system—in which these constraints must be considered. These constraints threaten to keep the TB target out of reach.

Inadequate resources and infrastructure

There is a shortage of both financial and human resources to combat TB in Kenya. The government health expenditure per capita for Kenya ($6) is well below the $35–$40 level estimated as necessary for providing essential services (CMH 2001). An even higher per capita level would be needed for scaling up and implementing new activities. The funding gap of $3.3 million for TB control activities in 2003 was not calculated considering the full range of additional activities that may be required to reach the Millennium Development Goals target, such as support of private sector DOTS delivery and targeted initiatives to reach the poor. Although funds from the GFATM will help decrease the gap over the next five years, a shortfall of finances will remain. Kenya's GFATM application for $4.9 million was a conservative request to ensure adequate absorption of award monies and did not include funding for major scaling up or expansion of activities. Furthermore, disbursement by the GFATM has been slow; to date, only the initial disbursement in August 2003 has been made. Delays in this process are likely to hinder the implementation of proposed activities that are necessary to reverse the trend in TB incidence.

Preservice training for nurses, clinical officers, and physicians is not consistent with the technical norms and operational guidelines of the NLTP, resulting in a considerable in-service training burden for the NLTP. A recent survey of patient treatment-seeking behavior found that most individuals with symptoms of TB visit public health facilities repeatedly before being appropriately referred for diagnosis (Hanson and Mansoer 2003). This suggests that even where access is possible, provider practice is often insufficient. In addition, careful case management, monitoring, and outreach for patients without a definitive treatment outcome are required to accurately determine the death rate and to return treatment interrupters to care. Outreach and case management activities are labor intensive but critical. Furthermore, as case detection improves (bringing more cases into the system) and as new initiatives and joint activities with the HIV/AIDS control program are rolled out, the need for additional staffing to implement these activities will become dire. The overall shortage and lack of appropriately trained human resources in the public health sector constrains the operations of the NLTP and will limit progress toward the target.

In 2003, there were 90 district coordinators in 74 districts overseeing more than 1,400 health units delivering TB control services. This number of coordinators is insufficient to support an expanded DOTS program that addresses private sector TB care, TB/HIV, and activities to reach the poor. Furthermore, these staff and their vehicles are often pulled from TB-related activities if outbreaks, other emergencies, or vaccination campaigns occur.

A 2003 survey of health workers identified the constraints or demotivating factors related to providing TB control services (NLTP 2003a). The most commonly cited complaint was the perception of being at increased risk of contracting TB. Workers suggested that a risk allowance or improved health insurance be offered to compensate for this risk. Among the top 10 requests were continuing education and training opportunities for health workers, and training of additional staff in TB control. A 1999 national survey of public health workers conducted as part of the Kenya Service Provision Assessment noted similar issues.

The HIV/AIDS epidemic

Modeling has been used to predict the effects of the HIV/AIDS epidemic on TB incidence. Modeling results indicate that achieving the global targets of 70 percent case detection and 85 percent treatment success rate will, at best, cause a slowing of the TB rate increase to approximately 7 percent per year (Elzinga, Raviglione, and Maher 2004). Therefore, achieving the global targets for case detection and treatment success alone is not enough to reverse the trend of TB incidence in populations with high HIV prevalence. Modeling based on Kenya-specific data of HIV prevalence among pregnant women and TB notifications in adults was used to project these rates up to the year 2015.[4] The results of this model suggest that if the current course is continued in Kenya, TB incidence will continue to rise. This model projects that the incidence of TB in Kenya can be halted or reversed only if HIV prevalence decreases.

Collaborative activities between TB and HIV/AIDS control programs are needed to accelerate the identification of TB patients and streamline access to TB and HIV/AIDS care. Kenya has developed plans conducting baseline surveys and for introducing TB/HIV collaborative activities and a joint TB/HIV coordinating body has been appointed. However, while these plans chart the NLTP on the correct course, implementing joint activities has not begun. There are insufficient human resources at the central level to propel this agenda, and ownership continues to rest predominantly with the NLTP. There is also the potential that this integration could result in redirecting human and financial resources from TB control to HIV/AIDS prevention and care if political commitment for TB control wanes.

Poverty

A healthy population is required for any country to move forward in its socio-economic development. Accordingly, key health concerns are typically included in a country's Poverty Reduction Strategy Paper (PRSP). A WHO report states that "PRSPs should prioritize those health interventions most likely to improve the health of the poor[est] and help to reduce poverty" (WHO 2004f). Although Kenya's 2000 Interim PRSP mentions the central role of HIV/AIDS control to effective poverty reduction, no reference is made to TB or its control, despite TB being a leading cause of death in AIDS patients.

In Kenya, where approximately 62 percent of the population lives on less than $2 a day, there is a significant association between the prevalence of poverty in a province and case detection rates, with the poorest provinces reporting the most cases (World Bank 2004). However, recent studies have suggested that the poor are underrepresented in the health system overall and in TB services specifically (World Bank 2001; Hanson and Mansoer 2003). This combination suggests that many of the "missing" cases are among the poor.

Issues of access

The health infrastructure in Kenya is relatively well developed, although equipment and staffing shortages mean that many facilities do not function optimally or at all. In addition, some important disparities between districts and between socioeconomic groups do exist. In the urban center of Nairobi, there are approximately 20 health facilities per 100,000 population while in the rural North Eastern Province there are only 8 facilities per 100,000.

A Welfare Monitoring Survey conducted in 1998 found that 88 percent of Kenyans sought care from formal sector providers, including pharmacies, during their last episode of illness. However, the 2003 Kenya Demographic and Health Survey found that less than 50 percent of mothers sought care from formal providers for their children with fever and symptoms of respiratory infection. This suggests that general access to the health system is not adequate. In addition provider practices are resulting in diagnostic delays and missed cases. Furthermore, the lack of reporting by the private sector, which delivers a considerable portion of the TB care in Kenya, likely accounts for much of the discrepancy between population coverage of 100 percent and case detection rates of 49 percent.

Private sector issues

Kenya has a growing private healthcare sector. TB care is delivered at a number of private hospitals, health centers, and dispensaries while private labs are providing smear microscopy services. Currently, 48 percent of all health facilities in Kenya are managed by the private and NGO sectors (Kenya 2001) while only 17 percent of the health facilities providing DOTS services are in these sectors.[5] Data from a recent facility-based survey suggested that TB patients sought care almost equally at public and private sector facilities (Hanson and Mansoer 2003). Private providers are those providing care outside of the formal public sector and may include traditional healers, pharmacists, qualified and unqualified practitioners, specialist physicians, private hospitals and nursing homes, and NGOs.

Studies from different countries have found TB management practices among private providers to be substandard (Stop TB and WHO 2003). Furthermore, data on TB patients diagnosed and treated in the private sector are likely not reported to the NLTP. In consideration of Kenya's low case detection rate and data on the use of private care by the poor, it is likely that many of the "missing cases" are receiving care in the private sector. Until guidelines and mechanisms for NLTP and private sector collaboration are developed, the case detection rate is likely to remain well below the 70 percent target.

Lack of community awareness

Since DOTS relies on passive case finding, general knowledge among the population about common TB symptoms and where to seek care is essential. Data from a behavioral study on TB conducted by PATH in 2000 showed a general awareness of TB and its seriousness to be widespread, but specific knowledge lacking about symptoms, transmission, and the potential for cure in the presence of HIV co-infection (PATH 2000). In addition, lengthy diagnostic delays were noted as patients often tried multiple home remedies, nonprescription medicines, and herbal or traditional therapies before presenting for medical care. Stigma was reported to exist within families, among healthcare providers, and in the community. Due to the frequency of co-morbidity, TB was often seen as a symptom of AIDS rather than a separate disease. A study funded by the World Bank found that only 17 percent of patients with TB symptoms who had accessed care knew that TB treatment was available free of charge through the public sector (Hanson and Mansoer 2003).

Recommended actions

Kenya has achieved great progress in its TB control efforts over the past decade. However, if Kenya remains on its current course, it will not reach the target by 2015. The extraordinary challenges Kenya is facing require extraordinary action. These recommended actions are urgently needed to accelerate Kenya's progress toward the goal of halting and reversing TB incidence.

Improving resources

Human resources development is critically needed. Strengthening human capacity at all NLTP levels is a key component of the WHO-led "Intensified Support and Action Countries" proposal that has been approved in principle by the Ministry of Health and is awaiting approval by the Directorate of Personnel Management (NTLP Kenya and KNCV Tuberculosis Foundation 2004). Prioritized activities include contracting additional provincial- and district-level supervisors in the AIDS belt of Kenya and in urban areas to assist with supervision, monitoring, and training; strengthening the Kenya Association for Prevention of Tuberculosis and Lung Diseases secretariat; and contracting a medical or clinical officer to assist with expanding public-private sector activities to other major cities. In addition, at the central level, a human resource development officer is needed to develop and implement a national TB Human Resource Development Plan, as well as a TB/HIV focal person to implement and monitor TB/HIV collaborative initiatives, and a TB/HIV national program officer at the Kenya WHO country office. International technical assistance focusing on human resource development and the components of the GFATM development plan including expanding TB/HIV, urban TB, and public-private sector activities is recommended under the Intensified Support and Action Countries proposal.

The Intensified Support and Action Countries proposal includes an incentive system linked to performance to motivate and recognize staff achievements. It is not just numbers of staff that are needed but also inculcating a better work ethic; targeting recruitment to attract qualified and motivated employees; ensuring appropriate levels of compensation; and developing clear and specific job descriptions, effective job aids, and strong supervision. Strengthening monitoring and evaluation of TB control activities is also a main objective of Kenya's GFATM proposal. Building capacity in monitoring, supervising, and evaluating must be a component of a comprehensive human resource development plan to ensure that quality services and program effectiveness are maintained. Prompt implementation of these activities will assist Kenya in rising to meet the challenge of human resources development.

The financial gap is well described in earlier sections. The $3.3 million funding gap for TB control activities must be closed and health expenditures per capita should be increased to $35–$45, a range that will cover scaling up activities necessary for achieving the TB target. However, the input of financial resources is limited by the absorptive capacity of the health system. Developing financial and human resources must be undertaken simultaneously to allow the effective use of both.

Tuberculosis and HIV collaborative activities

If Kenya is to reverse the rising trend in TB incidence, HIV/AIDS must be controlled too. Joint activities between TB and HIV/AIDS control programs must be stepped up. Intensified case finding among HIV-infected individuals and the use of isoniazid therapy to treat latent TB infection are planned. However, this still may not be enough to bring about a decline in TB case notifications. The introduction of antiretroviral medications on a broad scale is likely to have a significant impact on TB rates. If antiretrovirals are initiated when a patient has a CD4 count (an indicator of the damage done by the virus and the patient's ability to resist infection) of 200 cells per μl or less (and it is assumed that the median CD4 count at presentation of newly diagnosed TB patients in Kenya will be approximately 200 cells per μl), modeling experts predict that widespread use of antiretroviral therapy will prevent about 50 percent of the TB cases. If most patients are diagnosed with TB and HIV/AIDS concurrently, the beneficial effect of antiretroviral availability will be reduced. Therefore, more active case finding for HIV (which will allow antiretroviral therapy to be initiated before TB is diagnosed) will contribute to decreasing the incidence of TB.

Connect tuberculosis control to poverty reduction strategies

With additional support, a country's poverty alleviation plan may emerge as the primary investment strategy for the country. Priorities for health within the PRSPs and for TB within the health sector agenda will stimulate sustainable financing for TB as a core component of the country's development agenda. The links between TB and poverty in Kenya are evident. TB control programming must include interventions to target the poor. Directed interventions are needed to improve access to care in the public sector by removing hidden costs, raising awareness of TB symptoms and appropriate care options, and offering community-based care.

Improve access and services to capitalize on existing infrastructure

By shifting services to the district facility, decentralization can improve access to TB services. In addition, decentralization places increased decisionmaking and budgetary authority at the level where the care is provided—with the goal that care will be more accessible and acceptable to patients. In a study of decentralized TB care from the hospitals to the peripheral health units and the community within Machakos district in Kenya, treatment success rates for new smear-positive cases were found to be comparable (Kangangi and others 2003). Furthermore, in the decentralized setting, costs per patient fell and cost-effectiveness improved by 66 percent for new smear-positive cases (Nganda and others 2003).

Despite physically accessible primary healthcare services and overall high use, hidden costs to patients are the main reason for not using care. In the

Second Report on Poverty in Kenya, 40 percent of the poor who did not seek care for an illness reported it was because care was too expensive (while only 2.9 percent in rural areas reported being constrained by distance to a health facility) (Kenya 2002). The Ministry of Health recently waived fees for TB diagnostic examinations, which may improve TB service use by the poor. However, the issue of TB suspects not being referred promptly must also be addressed, since diagnostic delays can result in increased patient costs (in travel and time). Improving access to services is linked to human resource development to ensure free and swift diagnosis of TB patients.

The high TB case rates in urban areas will be addressed through a partnership of public and private sector physicians and pharmacists, prison authorities, and NGOs to expand and decentralize services in Nairobi. The number of diagnostic centers is expected to triple and the number of treatment facilities to double by the year 2006. With a grant from Fidelis, International Medical Corps is establishing TB diagnostic and treatment centers in the slum areas in Nairobi. If TB incidence can successfully be curtailed in Nairobi (where the greatest TB burden exists), this activity could have a significant effect on TB control in Kenya. If effective, scaling up this activity in Nyanza should be the next step.

Raise community awareness of tuberculosis

A national communication strategy is needed to address the issues of stigma, lack of knowledge about TB and care options, and, once diagnosed, to improve adherence to treatment. To this end, the Communication for Behavioral Impact plan was launched in Kenya in April 2004. Information, education, and communication materials, newspaper ads, radio announcements, and various circulars were used to inform the public about TB, including the availability of free diagnostic and treatment services. Public meetings at the district level, promotion of TB awareness in schools and improved sign posting of points of service are among the activities planned. However, just a month after its initiation, Communication-for-Behavioral-Impact was facing funding constraints and recognizing the need for additional capacity building and technical support. Full implementation of this broad-based national effort aimed at changing behaviors is a necessary contribution to reversing the incidence of TB in Kenya.

Establish public-private mix activities

Although the exact magnitude of private sector TB care is not known, TB cannot be controlled in Kenya without the involvement and collaboration of private sector providers. Successful pilot projects for engaging the private sector in DOTS have been launched in Nairobi and plans to extend these projects to other urban areas are under way. However, to rapidly scale up DOTS delivery by private sector providers, a more normative approach may be needed. DOTS must be promoted as the standard of care through existing forums such as those held by private associations and academic institutions.

Innovative measures such as the Health Franchising Initiative must be furthered. The Health Franchising Initiative uses social franchising to interest private providers, particularly those that treat the poor, in a franchising package. Private providers who become part of the franchise benefit from quality assurance, training, and access to free TB and AIDS drugs. Patients and the NLTP are assured that standardized, high-level care is provided. Furthermore, because the franchise members have declared themselves, the NLTP can ensure that TB data are collected from these providers and included in national reports. By improving access, linking TB and HIV care, developing human resources, targeting the poor, and closing the private provider loophole, this initiative will address multiple constraints simultaneously.

Conclusion

This case study outlines recommended actions to allow Kenya to reverse its current TB epidemiological trajectory and achieve a decline in its TB incidence. Many of the recommended activities are overlapping and interdependent—for example, human resources development is necessary for essentially every proposed activity, and mobilizing the private sector will help target services to the poor. Significant resources will be needed if Kenya is to set the example for other high-burden TB countries (particularly high-burden TB and HIV countries) and reach the TB target by 2015.

Recommended actions include:

- Improving resources:
  - Develop human resources—in both numbers and capacities.
  - Close the TB control funding gap.
- Step up TB/HIV collaborative activities—TB can only be controlled if HIV is also controlled.
- Connect TB control to poverty reduction strategies.
- Improve access and services to capitalize on existing infrastructure.
- Raise community awareness of TB.
- Establish and scale up public-private mix activities.

Tuberculosis and poverty in Cambodia

The Kingdom of Cambodia is a Southeast Asian country that borders Thailand, Lao PDR, and Viet Nam (map A3.1). The government of Cambodia is a multiparty democracy, formed on the basis of free elections. The population is largely Khmer, with Chinese and Cham minorities; more than 30 ethnic groups inhabiting the mountainous north and northeastern areas.[1]

The most recent census places the population at 13.5 million with over 1 million people living in the capital, Phnom Penh, and an overwhelming majority (81 percent) of the population living in rural areas. Based on criteria established in the national Poverty Reduction Strategy Paper, 36 percent of Cambodians live below the poverty line of $0.46–$0.63 a day (Cambodia 2002). The World Bank classifies Cambodia as a low-income, moderately indebted country.

The socioeconomic context

Life expectancy in Cambodia is 55.2 years for men and 59.5 for women. Children under age 15 make up 41 percent of the population; when the age marker is moved to age 20, the percentage swells to nearly 60 percent, making job prospects a major concern for the country's future.[2] The rate of unemployment reported in 2001 was 1.5 percent for men and 2.2 percent for women. More than 70 percent of Cambodians are employed in agricultural production and employment opportunities in secondary and tertiary sectors are limited.

Women are critically important to the economy of Cambodia: they constitute 54 percent of the skilled agriculture and fishery workers and make substantial contributions in nonagricultural sectors of economy. They contribute three-quarters of the primary labor force in wholesale and retail trade and two-thirds of the labor force in manufacturing. However, many of these jobs are part of the low-paying, informal sector and are especially vulnerable

Map A3.1

Cambodia: Population density, 2000

People per square kilometer

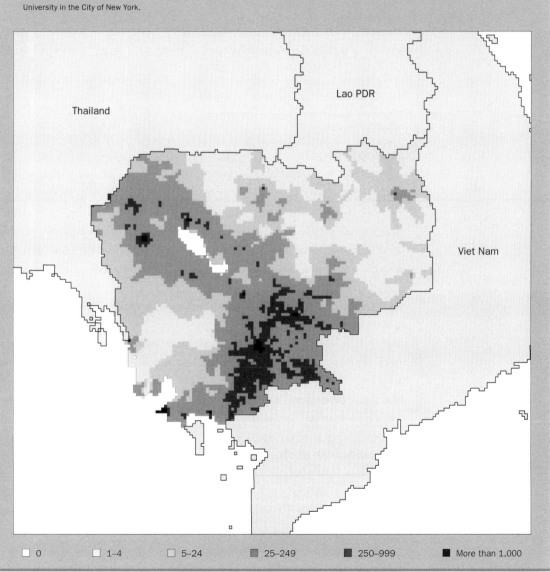

□ 0   □ 1–4   □ 5–24   ▨ 25–249   ▨ 250–999   ■ More than 1,000

Indicator	1996	2000	2001	2002
Births attended by skilled health staff	—	31.8	—	—
Health expenditure, private (share of GDP)	—	10.1	10	—
Health expenditure, public (share of GDP)	—	1.7	1.7	—
Health expenditure, total (share of GDP)	—	11.8	11.8	—
Immunization, DPT (share of children ages 12–23 months)	43	59	60	54
Improved sanitation facilities (share of population with access)	—	17	—	—
Improved water source (share of population with access)	—	30	—	—
Labor force, children ages 10–14 (share of age group)	—	23.7	23.5	23.4
Labor force, female (share of total labor force)	52.1	51.7	51.6	51.5
Literacy rate, adult total (share of people ages 15 and above)	65.1	68.0	68.7	69.4
Literacy rate, youth total (share of people ages 15–24)	76.3	79.1	79.7	80.2
Malnutrition prevalence, height-for-age (share of children under age 5)	53.3	44.6	—	—
Malnutrition prevalence, weight-for-age (share of children under age 5)	47.4	45.2	—	—
Unemployment, female (share of female labor force)	—	2.8	2.2	—
Unemployment, male (share of male labor force)	—	2.1	1.5	—

Table A3.1

Select health and social sector indicators: Cambodia

Percent

— not available

Source: World Bank 2004.

to exploitation. Women also experience higher rates of unemployment when compared with men. Access to education is markedly poorer for girls. This inequity grows as educational opportunities move into the secondary and tertiary levels (table A3.1).

The national Poverty Reduction Strategy Paper of Cambodia reflects an official acknowledgment of gender inequities. The plan's main strategies to address this inequity include ensuring that women and girls receive full legal protection, access to education about their rights and benefits, gender mainstreaming in all government departments, and collaboration with specific ministerial-level departments of health, education, agriculture, and rural income generation (Cambodia 2002).

Current health sector status

Efforts have been made to restore the health system, which was largely destroyed by the Khmer Rouge regime, but there are still significant obstacles to overcome to ensure that Cambodia's most neglected and vulnerable populations have access to health treatment, including the diagnosis and treatment of TB. The new health system established in the late 1990s operates at three levels and the health coverage plan is based on population and geography. Cambodians spend a high proportion of their average monthly expenditures on health. Public health services often carry fees that are unpredictable. People are often uncertain how much, when, and to whom they will have to pay, and whether or not basic resources will be consistently available. As a result, most people seek care in the private sector first or opt to self-treat. One survey showed that 70 percent of people who were recently ill initially went to the private sector, often buying their medicines in an unregulated pharmacy market (Cambodia 2002).

Tuberculosis in Cambodia

Cambodia is currently identified by the WHO as one of the 22 countries in the world that carry the highest burden of TB (figure A3.1). Accordingly, the Cambodian government has given TB a high level of political commitment in the midst of health sector reforms. Since the advent of the National Tuberculosis Control Program in 1980 and the establishment of DOTS in 1994, Cambodia has continued to work to alleviate the high burden of TB on society. The majority of individuals (69 percent) diagnosed with active TB in Cambodia are between the ages of 15 and 54 (figure A3.2) (WHO 2004g). For these individuals, the physical and economic impact of TB has negative, at times profoundly damaging, consequences on their ability to be economically productive and to care for their families during a time in their life when these activities would normally be a primary focus.

Young adults also experience the highest rates of HIV infection. Cambodia has made significant progress in its fight against HIV/AIDS, demonstrated by the sustained decrease in adult prevalence rates from over 4 percent to 2.6 percent in the past two years.[3] Despite successful efforts to slow HIV in Cambodia, TB/HIV co-infection will continue to be a challenging problem. Among adult TB cases, 14–20 percent are reported to also be infected with HIV (Marseille and Garbus 2002 WHO 2004h). In a recent survey of HIV-infected patients, 12 percent of 441 HIV-positive patients in Phnom Penh were diagnosed with active pulmonary TB using a single spot sputum specimen (both culture and smear) with a ratio of undetected to detected cases of three to one (Kimerling, Schuchter, and Chanthol 2002).

Since 1998, Cambodia has maintained a high DOTS population coverage with 100 percent coverage reported for 2002 (WHO 2004h). The creation of TB units and TB supervisors has facilitated this wide coverage. Seventy percent of the health centers now offer DOTS, with expansion to all of the 942 centers in the country anticipated by 2005. There is an urgent need, especially in the context of the HIV epidemic, to reduce the delay between the first symptoms and free access to DOTS. With decentralization of the health system, using the district-based health system may assist in accelerating the effort to detect 70 percent of the contagious TB cases while maintaining high standards of quality in treatment.

Some gains have been made in the estimated proportion of new smear-positive TB cases detected under DOTS, which is reported to be 52–57 percent and climbing (figure A3.3). This is felt to reflect programmatic improvements in case finding. This upward trend portends that the Millennium Development

Figure A3.1

**Cambodia:
Estimated TB
notification rate,
1980–2001**

Per 100,000 population

Note: SS+ is sputum smear
positive.

Source: WHO 2004j.

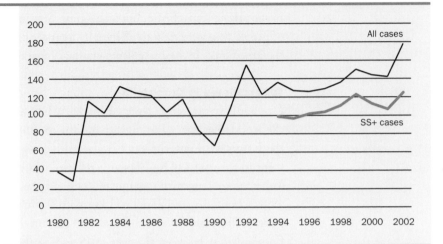

Figure A3.2

**Cambodia: Notification
rate of new sputum
smear–positive cases
by age and sex**

Source: WHO 2004j.

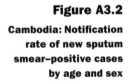

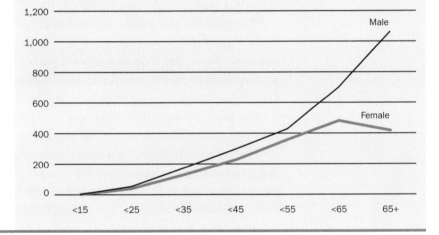

Figure A3.3

**Cambodia: Types of
TB cases notified**

Note: SS+ is sputum smear
positive. SS– is sputum smear
negative.

Source: WHO 2004j.

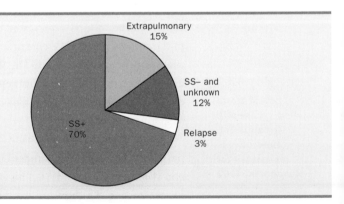

Goal target of exceeding 70 percent case detection by 2015 can be reached (UN Millennium Project 2004). The estimated prevalence of smear-positive tuberculosis (TB) per 100,000 population was 428 in 1997 and decreased to 311 in 2002. In spite of these successes, the TB death rate per 100,000 population rose from 90 in 1997 to 107 in 2002 (box A3.1) (WHO 2004h).

The number of health centers using DOTS increased from 9 in 1999, to 60 by the end of 2000, and to 706 by the end of 2003, highlighting the quick dissemination of the program. By the end of 2005, it is projected that there should be one DOTS facility per 10,000 population (a total of 145 TB units), which augments treatment provided by the 8 national hospitals, 68 referral hospitals, and 77 district hospitals (Cambodia 2001, 2003; Mao Tan Eang 2003).

The National Tuberculosis Control Program is coordinated through the National Center for TB and Leprosy Control (CENAT) and is chaired by the prime minister. Management capacity at the central level was reported to be satisfactory by the joint World Bank–WHO supervision mission in January 1999. The major objectives to be reached by 2005 are equity and access to TB services and a high cure rate (Cambodia 2001). The National Tuberculosis Control Program has prioritized policies for TB control that include free and accessible TB services, commitment to assuring an uninterrupted supply of supplies and good quality drugs, accurate reporting, and promotion of internal and external partnerships.

The government recognizes the economic impact of this disease on individuals and families. For example, the *Tuberculosis Report* prepared by the Ministry of Health in 2000 noted that TB patients lose an average of three to four months of work time and that the annual household income of a TB patient is reduced by 20–30 percent because of both the direct and indirect costs of the disease. In addition to the food given to all patients (TB or non-TB) by the government of Cambodia, additional food is supplied by the World Food Programme to TB patients in many regions of the country. This support plays an important role in promoting TB control activities such as increasing case finding, reducing defaulters, and maintaining the cure rate.

Box A3.1 Latest World Health Organization tuberculosis estimates for Cambodia, 2002		
Box A3.1	Global rank (based on estimated cases)	21
Latest World	Incidence (all cases per 100,000 population)	549
Health	Incidence (all sputum smear–positive cases per 100,000 population	242
Organization	Prevalence (all sputum smear–positive per 100,000 population)	311
tuberculosis	TB mortality (per 100,000 population)	107
estimates for	Percentage of adult (ages 15–49) TB cases that are also HIV-positive	14
Cambodia, 2002	Percentage of all new cases that are multidrug-resistant	4.2
Source: WHO 2004h.		

Current investment

Based on estimates for the 2003 fiscal year, the total TB control cost will be $9.0 million, of which $1.05 million will be covered by the National Tuberculosis Control Program budget. Costs not included in that budget that will be assumed by the government, such as hospital stays, clinic visits for DOTS patients, and TB monitoring, amount to $3.1 million. Although loans and grants from principal financial partners, including the World Bank, the Japan International Cooperation Agency, the Canadian International Development Agency, and the WHO, will provide $1.5 million, a funding gap of nearly $3.4 million persists.

With the approval of Cambodia's GFATM proposal in October 2003, $2.5 million was allocated to scale up TB control services over a two-year period. Furthermore, beginning in 2003, grant aid pledged by the government of Japan will ensure an uninterrupted supply of drugs. These funds will complement efforts of the Ministry of Health and the National Tuberculosis Control Program to expand DOTS, improve social mobilization and adult knowledge of TB, and strengthen monitoring and evaluation systems (Global Fund 2003a).

Systemic barriers to health services and DOTS access

- Widespread poverty. Impoverishment increases vulnerability to a wide range of illnesses, including TB, while creating financial and logistical obstacles to treatment access.
- Geographic isolation. The government estimates that 21 percent of the lowest quintile lives more than 5 kilometers from any health facility.
- Health personnel issues. Chronic personnel shortages and poor salary among health professionals are present throughout the country.
- Poor awareness of TB in the general population.
- Inconsistent and variable application of user fees in the public health system. Out-of-pocket spending on health by households accounts for 82 percent of total health spending. Poor families rely instead on home remedies and traditional healers, neither of which has ever demonstrated success in the treatment of TB (UN Millennium Project 2004).
- Consistency and quality of drug supply. The World Bank has estimated that 2,000 illegal pharmacies are providing poor-quality drugs and do not comply with Food and Drug Department regulations (UN Millennium Project 2004).

Recommendations

- Explicitly include scaled-up detection and treatment strategies for TB in the "Action Plan Matrix," recognizing it as a "Priority Poverty Reduction Action" within Cambodia's national Poverty Reduction Strategy

Paper. Include an assessment of the economic and social burden of this disease in Cambodia within the body of the plan.

- Expanded DOTS program and extended health center/health post capacity to conduct TB treatment at the community level, specifically targeting rural communities. Provide incentives to staff working in remote areas through performance-based measures.
- Remove economic barriers and address geographic isolation issues to improve access to the public health system.
- Increased budgetary allocation to fighting TB as well as more efficient use of those resources by expanding result-based management of the public health system.
- Strengthen involvement and communication with all health providers in public and private sectors. Establish official national standards for education and standards of professional practice.
- Strengthen collaboration between TB and HIV programs.
- Promote and sustain organizations for TB patients and their families within communities to provide mutual support during treatment and to serve as a center of advocacy and education efforts to reduce stigma. Collaborate with community elders, religious leaders, community health agents, and local health workers.
- Promote development and documentation of best practices that are specific to Cambodia and to the various ethnically diverse regions within the country. Issues addressed could include facilitating access for women within the context of larger constraints to their mobility that may presently exist, educating and integrating traditional healers, and addressing geographic access for isolated rural populations.

Tuberculosis and poverty in the Dominican Republic

The Dominican Republic encompasses two-thirds of the island of Hispaniola, situated between the Caribbean Sea and the North Atlantic. It is bordered on the west by the country of Haiti (map A4.1). The country has a long history of political turmoil, but since 1966 it has held regular, competitive elections. The 2004 elections, preceded by a period of significant political and economic unrest following the collapse of three of the country's largest banks, restored former president Leonel Fernandez to office.

The current population of the Dominican Republic is estimated at 8,873,000, with an annual growth rate of 1.5 percent. There has been a slow but steady decrease in the percentage of the population classified as rural, with current estimates at around 33 percent. The Dominican Republic is classified as a lower-middle income, less-indebted country by the World Bank. In 1998, official estimates placed 29 percent of the population below the poverty line. This situation is more dramatic in rural areas. In 1998, official figures showed that the poverty rate affected 46 percent of the rural population (World Bank 2004). In urban areas, 15 percent of the population lives below the poverty line. Per capita income figures do not give an accurate indication of actual status because of markedly skewed income shares within the population: the poorest 40 percent of the population receives less than 14 percent of the income share, while the richest 20 percent controls 53 percent. Additionally, a large number of Haitians (estimated at more than a million) who cross into the Dominican Republic seeking employment in the agricultural and service sectors remain undocumented and live in conditions of abject poverty with minimal or no access to health care or other social services.

The macroeconomic adjustments of the 1980s served to substantially reduce social spending and redirect expenditures toward investment, especially in infrastructure (PAHO 2001). Reduced public spending for education and

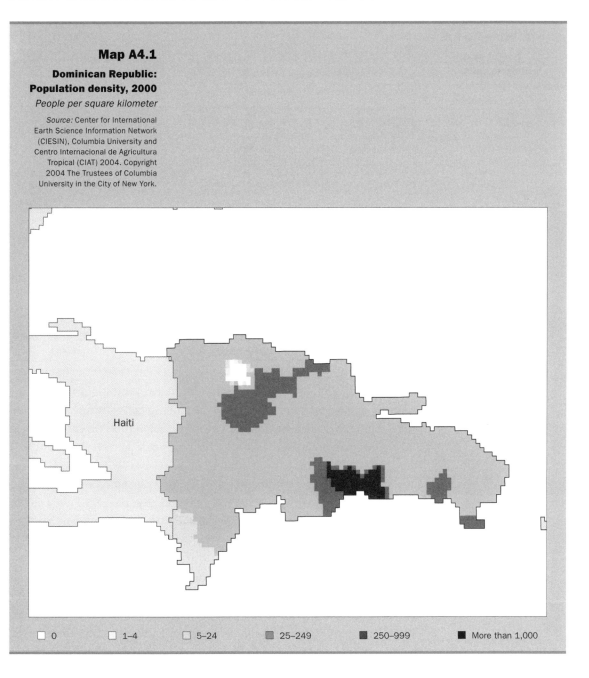

Map A4.1

Dominican Republic: Population density, 2000

People per square kilometer

Haiti

☐ 0   ☐ 1–4   ☐ 5–24   ■ 25–249   ■ 250–999   ■ More than 1,000

health has affected family budgets, unemployment rates, and the percentage of population linked to the informal economy and non–wage earning activities, and has thus led to a considerable increase in relative poverty and the number of people who are in need.

The socioeconomic context

Literacy is reported at 84 percent with a high (94 percent) rate of primary school completion. Women outnumber men in combined gross enrollment

Table A4.1

Select health and social sector indicators: Dominican Republic

Percent

— not available.

Source: World Bank 2004.

Indicator	1992	2000	2002
Births attended by skilled health staff	—	97.6	97.8
Expenditure, total education (share of GDP)	13.35	16.02	—
Health expenditure, private (share of GDP)	—	4	—
Health expenditure, public (share of GDP)	—	2.2	—
Health expenditure, total (share of GDP)	—	6.2	—
Improved sanitation facilities (share of population with access)	—	67	—
Improved water source (share of population with access)	—	86	—
Immunization, DPT (share of children ages 12–23 months)	73	68	72
Labor force, children ages 10–14 (share of age group)	—	13.22	12.04
Labor force, female (share of total labor force)	27.8	30.8	31.44
Literacy rate, adult total (share of adults ages 15 and above)	80.3	83.7	84.4
Literacy rate, youth total (share of people ages 15–24)	88.3	91.1	91.7
Malnutrition prevalence, height-for-age (share of children under age 5)	—	6.1	—
Malnutrition prevalence, weight-for-age (share of children under age 5)	—	4.6	—
Unemployment, female (share of female labor force)	34.9	23.3	—
Unemployment, male (share of male labor force)	11.7	8.7	—

throughout the primary and secondary educational institutions (tertiary not reported) and women are represented in government agencies and elected offices. However, the unemployment rate for women is three times that of men and women earn on average a third of the wages paid to men (UNDP 2003) (table A4.1). There are a large number of single-mother households in the Dominican Republic, and this decreased earning capability lowers the standard of living for these women and their children, compromising their ability to respond to a wide range of problems including health-related issues.

Current health sector status

According to the Public Health Code, the Secretariat for Public Health and Social Welfare is the agency in charge of health services and is responsible for applying the Code (PAHO 2001). The Secretariat provides health care, health promotion, and preventive health services and is structured on three levels: central, regional, and provincial. Eight regional offices direct the services and oversee the health areas, or units, at the provincial level. The health areas have rural clinics that each cover from 2,000 to 10,000 inhabitants and are staffed with medical interns or assistants, nurse's aides, a supervisor of health promoters, and the health promoters themselves.

The Secretariat's programs are structured at the central and regional levels. The most fully developed are those for the control of malaria, dengue, and other vector-borne diseases and for the prevention and control of rabies and zoonoses; the national TB program; immunization; family planning and reproductive health; and basic sanitation. There are epidemiological services at the national level and also units at the regional and local level. According to data from the Secretariat for Public Health, in 1996 there were a total of 1,334 health facilities in the country, of which 730 (55 percent) came directly under the Secretariat, 184 (14 percent) under the executive council of the Dominican Social Security Institute (an autonomous institution that covers risks from disease, disability, old age, death, and on-the-job accidents incurred by employed workers), 417 (31 percent) under the private sector, and 3 (0.2 percent) under the armed forces. The bed to population ratio is 1 to 500. However, there is a discrepancy among different sources on the number of beds available.

Tuberculosis in the Dominican Republic

Communicable diseases, along with nutritional deficiencies, are identified as the country's leading health priorities. In 1994 communicable diseases accounted for 16.8 percent of all diagnosed deaths (the largest category within infectious diseases was diarrheal diseases, particularly in infants and young children). Tuberculosis (TB) accounted for 2 percent of all diagnosed deaths and 15 percent of the deaths from communicable diseases. Few vaccine-preventable diseases were diagnosed as causes of death. Since 1992 there has been a steep decline in mortality due to these diseases. Tubercular meningitis continues to decline, with an incidence of less than 1 per 100,000 population in 1996 (PAHO 2001).

In the Dominican Republic (as in many countries of the world), the highest rate of TB infection is among young adults. This coincides with what should be a time of prime economic and reproductive activity. However, instead of earning wages, developing sustainable subsistence, and providing for their young families, victims of TB, AIDS, and a host of other treatable and preventable diseases are faced with serious, expensive illnesses that will frequently cause them (and their families) to cycle deeper into poverty.

In their recent application to the Global Fund to Fight AIDS, Tuberculosis, and Malaria (2003b), the Dominican Republic summarized the current TB situation:

> Over the past two decades, the National Tuberculosis Control Program has reported morbidity rates of approximately 50 cases per 100,000 inhabitants. The rates recorded over these years have not been constant. This is related with under-recording of 50 percent, according to PAHO/WHO estimates [WHO estimates a 149/100,000 prevalence]. The incidence rate recorded for 2002 was 43.8/100,000, which translates as 3,682 new cases, of which 59 percent correspond to BK+ [smear-positive] pulmonary cases (2,176), giving a rate of 25.9/100,000 inhabitants. The actions of the National Tuberculosis Control Program to apply the DOTS strategy in health establishments are promising [see figures A4.1, A4.2, and A4.3 for features of TB in the Dominican Republic].

Figure A4.1

Dominican Republic: Estimated TB notification rate, 1980–2001

Per 100,000 population

Note: SS+ is sputum smear positive.

Source: WHO 2004j.

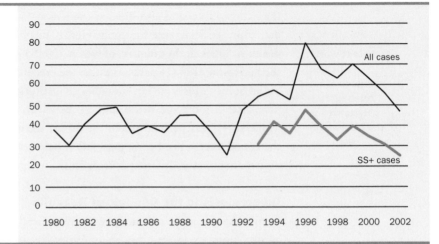

Figure A4.2

Dominican Republic: Notification of new sputum smear–positive cases by age and sex

Source: WHO 2004j.

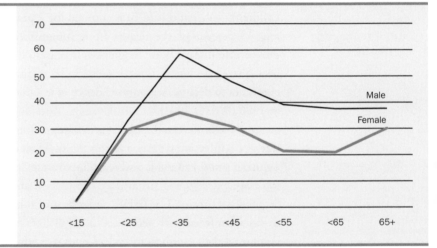

Figure A4.3

Dominican Republic: Types of TB cases notified

Note: SS+ is sputum smear positive. SS– is sputum smear negative.

Source: WHO 2004j.

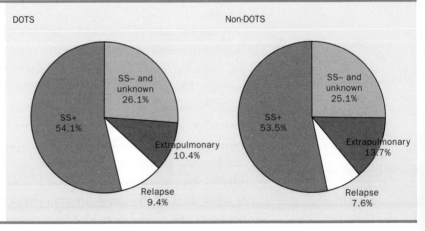

Box A4.1

Latest World Health Organization tuberculosis estimates for the Dominican Republic

Source: WHO 2004j.

Global rank (based on estimated cases)	82
Incidence (all cases per 100,000 population)	95
Incidence (all sputum smear–positive cases per 100,000 population)	42
Prevalence (all sputum smear–positive per 100,000 population)	56
TB mortality (per 100,000 population)	18
Percentage of adult (ages 15–49) TB cases that are also HIV positive	13
Percentage of all new cases that are multidrug resistant	6.6

DOTS coverage is now reported to be at 71 percent (WHO 2003d). In non-DOTS areas, treatment is mainly self-administered by patients, many of whom receive it irregularly. It is important to point out that the low level of direct smear confirmation reflects the poor functioning of the laboratory network.

The greatest disease burden is borne by highly vulnerable populations living under conditions of poverty and extreme poverty, such as the population of Haitian immigrants, the populations of the highly impoverished *bateyes* (sugar plantation workers, their families and, with increasing frequency, unemployed workers), and the prison population; groups that are also affected by the growing tendency of the HIV/AIDS epidemic, with co-infection present in 5.4 percent of the TB cases recorded last year. The HIV prevalence rate is 2.3 percent, and HIV/AIDS is now the leading cause of death among women of reproductive age in the Dominican Republic (UNAIDS 2002). The high HIV prevalence rate is evident in the growing TB incidence, with the Dominican Republic showing five times the number of active cases than is found on average in Latin America (box A4.1).

Since 1983, when the first case of AIDS was reported in the Dominican Republic, the incidence of this disease has risen annually. Current efforts to address the growing TB incidence are closely linked with the ongoing effort to actively address the HIV/AIDS crisis in the Dominican Republic. As is the case throughout most of the world, TB is the largest opportunistic infection for people living with AIDS.

Although the Dominican Republic is not classified as one of the high-burden TB countries overall, the rate of TB is significant, and along with HIV/AIDS infections continues to grow. The proportion of mycobacterium TB strains resistant to one or more drugs in the Dominican Republic is among the highest observed worldwide. The most frequent causes of multidrug-resistant tuberculosis (MDR-TB) are identified as inadequate treatment and poor completion rates. The response to MDR-TB requires detailed laboratory monitoring; extended, uninterrupted treatment (at times, treatment time is as long as two years); and reliable drug supplies. MDR-TB is more costly to treat and patients can experience significant side effects from the second- and third-line treatment regimens.

An ongoing surveillance project, begun in 1997, entitled Anti-Tuberculosis Drug Resistance in the World, has been conducted by the International Union Against Tuberculosis and Lung Disease (IUATLD) and the World Health Organization (WHO) along with several national and international partners. The last study in which detailed surveys from the Dominican Republic were available was the report covering 1994–97, first published in the *New England Journal of Medicine* in 1998 (Pablo-Mendez and others 1998). This study identified the Dominican Republic as an MDR-TB "hotspot" with 6.6 percent of TB patients showing multidrug resistance. The same report documented that the Dominican Republic had the highest rate (42.2 percent) of combined resistance to any one of the four TB drugs tested (Pablo-Mendez and others 1998).

Current investment

In February of 2004, the World Bank approved a $100 million Social Crisis Response Adjustment Loan targeted at reducing the social impact of the current economic crisis in the Dominican Republic. One of the projected uses of the loan is to extend health insurance to all. Additional budgetary support will be needed to develop the underfunded health system and to expand the DOTS. The total healthcare spending in the Dominican Republic represents only 6 percent of the gross domestic product per year, which is below the average for Latin America and the Caribbean.

From the Global Fund application:

Up until February 2002, the [TB] Program operated with a limited budget and resources allocated by the State Secretariat for Public Health and Social Welfare (SESPAS), as part of the national budget, to cover payment of technical personnel and purchase of medicines and laboratory consumables, which also had limited distribution. Since then, with the signature of an agreement to implement the Project to Strengthen the National Tuberculosis Program and Reduce the Impact of Association with HIV/AIDS in the Dominican Republic, [$] 1,119,000 has been received from USAID to extend the DOTS strategy to the 8 areas of the National District and 7 provinces prioritized because of the notified burden of the disease, HIV-AIDS association, etc. This project will be extended to another 3 provinces in the next stage, in 2004.

[The] proposal to the Global Fund aims to respond to TB control in the 20 provinces and vulnerable groups with a high TB burden and double HIV-AIDS infection, where TB control activities are currently being implemented with the very limited resources that the SESPAS funding allows, in a very complex, hard-to-access territory, where external funding for 2002 consisted of USD 44,000 from the World Bank. These resources have been used for small health personnel training activities in provinces not supported by the USAID project. [The Global Fund proposal] would allow countrywide DOTS strategy coverage, co-funded 58% by SESPAS, 22% by the Global Fund, 18% by USAID and 2% by the World Bank.

Systemic barriers to health services and DOTS access

- Significant numbers of people living in poverty. The direct and indirect costs of disease and illness can cause impoverishment and increase the depth of poverty for individuals and their families.
- DOTS coverage not completely integrated throughout the system.
- Health staff shortages and lack of systematic training of health personnel in administering DOTS.
- Large numbers of undocumented, vulnerable immigrants.
- Inadequate laboratory facilities and inadequate quality assurance in existing facilities.
- A minimal number of staff trained in administering DOTS.
- Seasonal transportation obstacles.

Recommendations

The goal is reducing the burden of TB in the Dominican Republic including detection in and treatment of the most vulnerable populations (Haitian immigrants, prison inmates, and the population of the *bateyes*). Overall detection rates are still below 60 percent and DOTS detection rates are at 43 percent. Focused attention is needed to rise above 70 percent and to reach the Millennium Development Goal target of decreasing prevalence and deaths by 2015.

The following recommendations are drawn from a variety of sources.

- Promote poverty reduction through the expanding coverage and quality of education and improving access to quality health care.
- Explicitly include the social and economic impact of TB as well as the targeted actions and resources needed to treat it in poverty reduction strategies.
- Aggressively extend and consolidate the DOTS strategy to all existing health facilities with focused attention on local outreach to and accessibility for vulnerable population groups.
- Develop and maintain an equitable and consistent compensation structure for health workers.
- Enhance the diagnosis network. Reorder and coordinate TB diagnosis laboratories as a vital complement to attain the cure and diagnosis goals raised by WHO/PAHO for 2005. This will include acquiring necessary equipment; systematic and monitored quality control; and

ongoing staff education both in the larger primary system and the National Tuberculosis Control Program.

- During the projected expansion of the number of labs, also include the training and equipment necessary to diagnose MDR-TB so that when the DOTS programs are firmly in place and functioning consistently, DOTS-Plus can be rapidly incorporated into the existing system.
- Increase healthcare per capita spending. Address logistical and financial barriers to health services.
- Accelerate and coordinate response to patients co-infected with TB and HIV.
- Target outreach and education assistance for women who are single heads of households.
- Develop and document "best practices" operational research to identify things that work within the specific context of the Dominican Republic and then to conduct formalized operational research so that the information can be utilized throughout the country. Reinforce and improve the information system of the National Tuberculosis Control Program.

Tuberculosis and poverty in Ethiopia

The Federal Democratic Republic of Ethiopia is a landlocked country in the horn of Africa (map A5.1). The Ethiopian People's Revolutionary Democratic Front took control in 1991 after years of political instability, bloodshed, and drought. The constitution was ratified in December 1994 and the first multiparty elections were held in 1995. The current president, Girma Wolde-Giorgis Lucha, was elected for a six-year term in 2001.

The population of Ethiopia for 2004 is estimated at 72.4 million people with an annual growth rate of 2.4 percent. An overwhelming 84 percent live in frequently isolated rural areas with a strong reliance on agriculture for economic security. However, due to frequent droughts and lack of long-term sustainable cultivation practices, such dependence on agriculture has led to a nation with little guarantee of a consistent food supply and a scarcity of reliable employment. Over 44 percent of the population lives below the national poverty line.

Ethiopia has been classified as a low-income, severely indebted country by the World Bank and holds the status of a least developed country in the United Nations. By 2001, Ethiopia's debt stood at 65.6 percent of its gross domestic product (GDP). In 2004, the International Monetary Fund and the World Bank's International Development Association concluded that Ethiopia qualified for debt alleviation due to its strong progress with the Heavily Indebted Poor Countries Initiative.

The socioeconomic context

Life expectancy in Ethiopia (currently 43 years for women and 41.3 years for men) has been slowly declining since 1990. Unemployment is high and about 82 percent of the population (almost 60 million people) in Ethiopia subsist on less than a dollar a day, with the lowest quintile controlling only 2.4 percent

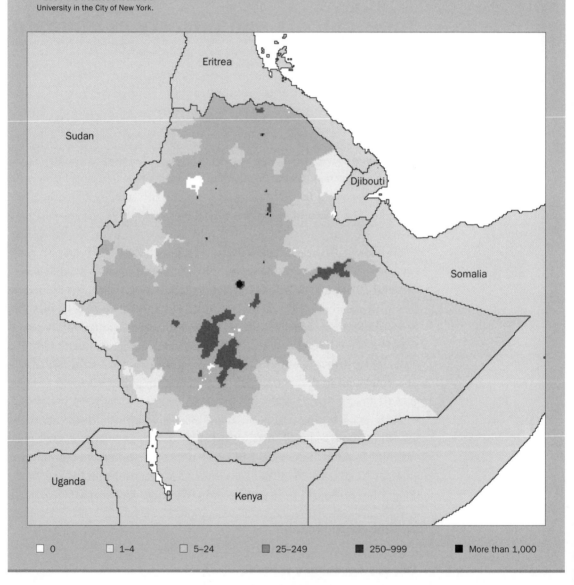

Map A5.1

Ethiopia: Population density, 2000

People per square kilometer

Source: Center for International Earth Science Information Network (CIESIN), Columbia University and Centro Internacional de Agricultura Tropical (CIAT) 2004. Copyright 2004 The Trustees of Columbia University in the City of New York.

□ 0   □ 1–4   □ 5–24   ■ 25–249   ■ 250–999   ■ More than 1,000

Year	1992	1999	2000	2002
Births attended by skilled health staff	—	—	5.6	—
Health expenditure, private (share of GDP)	—	2.2	2.1	—
Health expenditure, public (share of GDP)	—	1.3	1.1	—
Health expenditure, total (share of GDP)	—	3.5	3.2	—
Immunization, DPT (share of children ages 12–23 months)	13	21	56	56
Malnutrition prevalence, height-for-age (share of children under age 5)	64.2	—	51.5	—
Malnutrition prevalence, weight-for-age (share of children under age 5)	47.7	—	47.2	—
Improved sanitation facilities (share of population with access)	—	—	12	—
Improved water source (share of population with access)	—	—	24	—
Labor force, children ages 10–14 (share of age group)	—	41.34	41.1	40.638
Labor force, female (share of total labor force)	40.86	40.88	40.9	40.96
Literacy rate, adult total (share of people ages 15 and above)	30.58	37.96	39.10	41.5
Literacy rate, youth total (share of people ages 15–24)	45.38	53.78	54.99	57.4
Unemployment, female (share of female labor force)	—	12.5	—	—
Unemployment, male (share of male labor force)	—	4.3	—	—
Expenditure, total education (share of GDP)	17.83	26.62	—	—

Table A5.1

Select health and social sector indicators: Ethiopia

Percent

— not available.

Source: World Bank 2004.

of the income share (World Bank 2004). Adult literacy rates for men are at 49 percent and at 34 percent for women, with only a small percentage of the population (19 percent for boys, 11 percent for girls) completing primary school (World Bank 2004). One study conducted in southwest Ethiopia concluded that an increasing proportion of the child population is being taken out of schools and put into the labor force, both paid and unpaid, in order to contribute to family earnings and productivity (Aberra, Kifle, and Indrias 2003).

Women play an important role in the economy of Ethiopia, consistuting over 40 percent of the workforce. However, the unemployment rate for women is three times the rate for men. Educational disparities between men and women are evident on all three (primary, secondary, and tertiary) levels with the number of men enrolled consistently outnumbering the number of women. The gender gap widens as the educational level advances, with approximately twice as many men as women in the tertiary system (World Bank 2004).

Current health sector

Ethiopia has undergone major political and economic transitions since 1991, including widespread health sector reform. In 1997, as part of a 20-year Health Sector Investment Program, the first Health Sector Development Plan was launched to respond to emerging health problems. In particular, this plan addressed gender issues and the organization of appropriate healthcare delivery mechanisms to pastoralist communities (Ethiopia 1998). Although the policy had many positive outcomes—including a rise in potential health coverage from 33 percent to 52 percent, an increased immunization coverage rate from 20 percent to 42 percent, and an increase in the number of government and NGO Health Facilities providing DOTS—the Ethiopian government realized this plan was not reaching people at the grassroots level as well as it had hoped (Ethiopia 2003a). Furthermore, they concluded that a stronger attack on poverty-related diseases was necessary (Ethiopia 1998).

Tuberculosis in Ethiopia

Ethiopia is classified as one of the world's 22 high-burden countries for tuber-culosis (TB) with a WHO-estimated incidence of all cases at 370 per 100,000 population. The chronic high rates of malnutrition (worsened by recent, severe droughts), overcrowding, physical stress, emotional anxiety, and one the world's highest national rates of HIV infections (adult HIV prevalence is 5.4 percent) have created a formidable environment in which TB has and will continue to proliferate (Ethiopia 2003b). Yet there is no mention of TB and its social and economic burden in the Sustainable Development and Poverty Reduction Program Report.

HIV, like TB, is concentrated in the young, economically and reproduc-tively active population segment. Within this 15–24 age group, HIV prev-alence among women is three times greater than among men and mother-to-child transmission contributes to the second highest number of new HIV infections each year (USAID 2003). An estimated 30 percent (rural) to 60 percent (urban) of adult TB patients are HIV positive (WHO 2004i, Bruch-feld and others 2002). The Ethiopian government has set up a national TB/HIV coordinating body, and plans include providing antiretroviral therapy to TB/HIV co-infected patients in 2004.

At the same time as the launch of the second Health Sector Development Plan in 2002–03, a 2002–06 mid-term Strategic Plan for TB Control based on the DOTS strategy was integrated into the general health services. Health sector reform, carried out within the framework of the Health Sector Devel-opment Plan, is in line with the integration of TB treatment into the general health services and is progressively decentralizing service delivery to peripheral health units in *woredas*. However, more than half of the Ethiopian popula-tion lives farther than 10 kilometers from the nearest health facility. Although DOTS expansion has been facilitated by the decentralization of TB care and the expansion of at least one DOTS center in 86 percent of the *woredas*, many of the *woredas* are so large that a more accurate estimate would be about 40 percent of the population with true access (WHO 2004i).

Ethiopia has attempted to take an aggressive approach to TB prevention and treatment, but lack of resources for social sector programs and person-nel recruitment limits will continue to impede the ability to respond to this crisis on an appropriate scale. The Ethiopian government's commitment to such services can be seen in the continuous increase in notification rates from 1998 to 2002 (figure A5.1), as well as the increase in the number of centers that offer DOTS. In part, this is attributed to improved cooperation between the Tuberculosis and Leprosy Control Program (TLCP) and the general health sector in which it is now situated. However, DOTS case detection rates have been less than 50 percent in the past years, far below the global target of 70 percent and the number of cases notified by the NTLP continues to be significantly less than the WHO estimates of cases (figures A5.2 and A5.3) (WHO 2004i). The HIV epidemic will continue to drive the TB epidemic, with almost 30 percent of the people diagnosed with TB also found to be HIV positive (box A5.1).

Current government and donor investment

The Ethiopian government spent 3.6 percent of its GDP on health in 2001 (World Bank 2004). Five percent of this health expenditure was used for TB (GFATM 2002). The total TB control cost for the 2003 fiscal year was $14.2 million, though only $10.6 million was included in the TB budget. The Ethiopian government's total contribution to the budget was $2.2 million, which reflects an increase of $1.1 million over 2002. This funded staff working exclusively for TB control and contributed to the costs of buildings, equipment, and vehicles. The government also covered costs ($3.6 million) not included in the budget, including patient hospital stays and clinic visits for DOT and monitoring. The remaining money ($8.4 million) came from grants. The Global Fund to Fight AIDS, Tuberculosis, and Malaria (GFATM) has committed nearly $11 million to Ethiopia over a two-year period between 2003 and 2004. GFATM hopes these actions will increase smear-positive case detection rates from the current 36 percent to 55 percent and increase the treatment success rate from 81 percent to the Millennium Development Goal target of 85 percent within the two years. Ethiopia also has many key partnerships with NGOs as well as with governments from other countries. These alliances have helped with monetary, technical, and operational support for TB programs throughout the country.

Box A5.1		
Latest	Global rank (based on estimated cases)	7
World Health	Incidence (all cases per 100,000 population)	370
Organization TB	Incidence (all sputum smear–positive cases per 100,000 population)	159
estimates for	Prevalence (all sputum smear–positive per 100,000 population)	265
Ethiopia, 2002	Tuberculosis mortality (per 100,000 population)	88
Source: WHO 2004j.	Percentage of adult (15–49) TB cases that are also HIV positive	29
	Percentage of all new cases that are multidrug resistant	2.3

Figure A5.1

Six-year trend in case detection rates versus case notification rates in Ethiopia

Note: TLCP is Tuberculosis and Leprosy Control Program. SS+ is sputum smear positive.

Source: WHO 2004j.

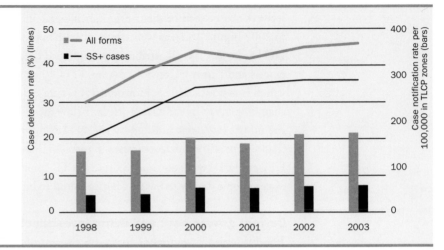

Figure A5.2

Gap between WHO estimates for Ethiopia and actual cases notified by TLCP

Number of cases (thousands)

Note: TLCP is Tuberculosis and Leprosy Control Program. SS+ is sputum smear positive.

Source: WHO 2004j.

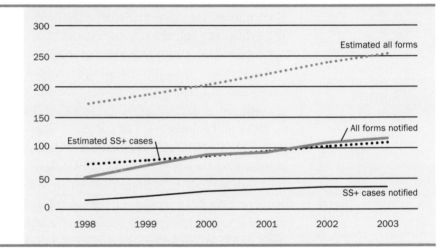

Figure A5.3

Case notification rates in Ethiopia, 1998–2003

Cases reported (thousands)

Note: Numbers above bars are total cases registered. PTB+ is pulmonary TB smear positive, PTB- is pulmonary TB smear negative, EPTB is extrapulmonary TB, R/F/D is relapse/failure/default.

Source: WHO 2004j.

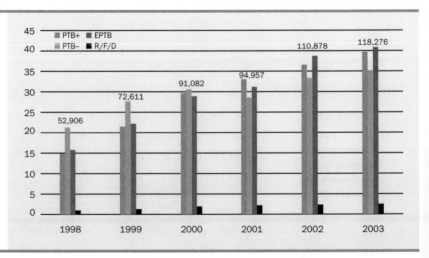

Community investment in tuberculosis control

Realizing that, even with 100 percent health facility coverage, the actual population coverage for TB services will be less due to limited access, TLCP has acknowledged the need for structural involvement of the community. Currently four *woredas* in four regions will begin community TB case care based on a national proposal that provides the details for community involvement in TB control as well as associated guidelines and training modules. The characteristics of such involvement include the participation of community members in raising awareness about TB, assisting and supporting DOTS and identifying TB suspects in the community, thus enhancing case detection and treatment adherence.

TB clubs, organized by community members, have emerged as an innovative tool for supporting TB patients at the *kebele* (smallest administrative area of a district) level (Getahun and Maher 2000). Clubs are formed by TB patients living in the same area; generally each club has 3–10 members. They offer support to one another and help identify additional people in the community with suspected TB. One study in two rural districts in the north demonstrated that quantifiable benefits from the clubs were discernible with improved rates of treatment completion and reduction of patients who default (Demissie, Getahu, and Lindtjorn 2003). In addition, the clubs help with TB education in their *kebeles* using materials provided by the Ministry of Health.

Systemic barriers to health services and DOTS access

- Widespread, profound poverty. Impoverishment increases vulnerability to a wide range of illnesses, including TB, while concurrently creating financial and logistical obstacles to treatment access.
- Geographic isolation. Only 12 percent of the roads are paved and over 50 percent of Ethiopia's population lives more than 10 kilometers from the closest health facility (WHO 2004i).[1]
- Underuse of available resources. Slow budget approvals and slow distribution of funds impedes program development and expansion (Ethiopia 2003a).
- Health staff shortages. With ratios of doctors and health officers to patients of 1 to 28,339 and nurses to patients of 1 to 5,236, the shortage of workers continues to have a critical, negative impact (Ethiopia 2003a).
- Variable rates of decentralization. Many rural areas remain inoperable and without adequate staffing, equipment, drugs and other supplies, and supervision mechanisms.
- Quality assurance problems in laboratories. These problems are attributed to inadequate supervision and monitoring. A program to ᵈʳᵉss these deficiencies has been instituted in four regions (WHO 2

Recommendations

- Explicitly include the social and economic impact of TB in the Poverty Reduction Strategy Paper. Include detection and treatment strategies as specific objectives in "Targets" and "Key Actions" of the plan.
- Increase health expenditure per capita.
- Remove economic barriers and address geographic barriers that limit access to the health system.
- Lift health sector recruitment restrictions and spending limits. Design and implement a plan for recruitment, retention, and training of staff at all levels, including increases in staff compensation and benefits. Train and use paid community health workers.
- Expand DOTS, and the necessary support infrastructure, to all existing health facilities and develop a plan to ensure adequate transportation to such facilities.
- Continue to strengthen the collaboration between the TB and HIV programs.
- Continue expanding the "Health Extension Package" beyond the original five regions of Oromia, Tigray, Amhara, South Ethiopia Peoples' State, and Dire Dawa. Explicitly incorporate TB education into this program.
- Create dedicated position(s) within the TLCP to develop and implement focused, supported plans to engage both rural and urban communities in TB awareness campaign (McCoy and others 2003).
- Promote the development of community-based TB services and support networks, such as TB clubs, in remote areas that have limited access to health facilities.
- Engage employers on the issue of TB and its impact on their workforce.
- Promote program-based operational research, including an appraisal of the local barriers to TB services and proposed interventions to overcome them. Develop and document best practices that are specific to Ethiopia.

Public-private partnerships for new tuberculosis diagnostics, drugs, and vaccines: Aeras, FIND, and the Global Alliance for TB Drug Development

Several new public-private partnerships have been established to develop the new tools necessary to effectively combat TB throughout the world.

Aeras (vaccines)

The Aeras Global TB Vaccine Foundation (http://www.aeras.org/) was founded as the Sequella Global Tuberculosis Foundation in 1997 to help develop new concepts and tools to control the global TB epidemic. In 1999 the foundation received a five-year $25 million grant from the Bill & Melinda Gates Foundation to fund the TB Vaccine Collaboration. Now the organization focuses solely on developing new vaccines against TB and ensuring their availability to all who need them. In February 2004, the Bill & Melinda Gates Foundation awarded Aeras a grant of $82.9 million for new tuberculosis (TB) vaccine development.

Although TB can be treated with drugs, the basic therapeutic regimen requires at least six months to complete and as many as four different drugs need to be taken. In combination with drug therapy, a moderately effective vaccine against TB could substantially reduce the disease burden. An existing TB vaccine, Bacillus Calmette-Guerin (BCG) has been in use since early in the twentieth century and is administered to millions of newborns around the world; it is thought to be effective in the first few years of life against severe TB disease. Better vaccination for TB that would protect against the disease in children and adults is urgently needed.

It is the goal of Aeras to develop, test, characterize, license, manufacture, and distribute a new TB vaccine within 10 years. Aeras will give special priority to promising prime-boost regimens of vaccine candidates that have a high probability of success for inducing protection against TB, achieving li sure, and being manufactured on a large scale at a reasonable cost. C candidate vaccines include recombinant BCG vaccines and novel recombinant, fusion proteins given with novel adjuvants.

Aeras performed the preclinical evaluation and regulatory activities for a new recombinant BCG vaccine candidate and launched a Phase I trial in February 2004. Aeras has worked for several years with the University of Cape Town to establish a clinical research site in Cape Town, South Africa, where a Phase IV BCG trial has enrolled more than 10,000 individuals. This site, along with a new site being developed in southern India, will be used for Phase II and Phase III trials of candidate vaccines.

FIND (diagnostics)

FIND Diagnostics (www.finddiagnostics.org/) has been established to address the critical need for accurate, rapid, and affordable diagnostic tests for infectious diseases, which account for nearly half of all deaths in developing countries. FIND was established with funding from the Bill and Melinda Gates Foundation. A grant of $30 million for the first five years of the project provides for a concerted research effort in collaboration with academia and industry with the aim of delivering affordable, simple diagnostics for the priority needs of developing countries.

Driven by the huge burden of disease, the existence of global control strategies and the capacity to treat detected patients, FIND has selected TB as its initial disease focus. Improved diagnostic tools are critical for both public and individual health. A lack of access to appropriate diagnostic tools in areas where resources are inadequate is a key contributor to the continuing transmission and incidence of disease and an increase in disease burden.

More than 100 years after its invention, microscopic examination of sputum is still the only widely available diagnostic tool for TB in developing countries. The lack of sensitivity of this technique for noninfectious cases, compounded by the difficulty of maintaining well equipped laboratories to perform it, means that only a fraction of patients with TB symptoms will currently get an accurate laboratory diagnosis.

Accurate and early detection is critical to an integrated approach to managing both the spread and the treatment of disease. Although much progress has been made in providing affordable treatment, the ability to treat a disease is only as good as the ability to diagnose it. The relatively poor performance of TB diagnostic tests leaves large numbers of infected patients undetected, erodes faith in public health services, impedes the expansion of DOTS, increases morbidity, and, most importantly, allows continued transmission of disease.

Delivery of improved TB diagnostic tests to high-burden countries will enable increased numbers of infected individuals to be identified, thus allowing for expansion of appropriate treatment programs. In addition to improving case detection, new diagnostic tools are also urgently needed to enable rapid testing of a patient's susceptibility to anti-TB drugs and to detect latent TB infection. This will also allow for more appropriate use of treatment resources and less potential for the development and spread of multidrug-resistant strains of TB. Currently, most patients with multidrug-resistant tuberculosis (MDR-TB) are not identified until they have failed one or more courses of conventional therapy over a period of months (or years). The result is increased morbidity, the selection of drug-resistant populations of bacteria, and the continued transmission of multidrug-resistant strains.

Technology exists that has the ability to vastly improve detection rates of TB, but this has been widely used only in affluent societies, where the impact on disease control is evident. The current approach taken by industry in developing diagnostic tests focuses predominantly on the research, development, and evaluation phases. FIND has developed and is focusing on a strategic approach that will move promising technology, for which clear proof of principle exists, into clinical evaluation and up to policy impact in the public sector of high-burden countries. The FIND vision is to translate these technological and scientific advances into easy-to-use and affordable tools for the benefit of the underprivileged in developing countries.

As an independent, not-for-profit organization, FIND works with the private sector, where better diagnostics are being developed, and the public sector, where much of the regulation of diagnostics and strategy for addressing neglected diseases is focused.

FIND invests primarily in late-stage development of diagnostic tests, investing in optimizing or re-engineering the technology, undertaking the necessary clinical trials to prove efficacy and proof of cost-effectiveness to support wide-scale use. To ensure successful implementation in developing countries, FIND aims to demonstrate product performance and impact on disease control efforts. Through their Intellectual Property Management strategy, FIND assists in ensuring that those countries that most need these tests gain affordable access. FIND's public health–driven mission ensures that the diagnostic needs of the developing world are met without being hindered by commercial interests.

The Global Alliance for TB Drug Development (new drugs)

The TB Alliance (http://www.tballiance.org/) is a nonprofit public-private partnership accelerating the discovery and development of new, faster acting, and affordable TB medicines. A lead research agency of the Stop TB Partnership, the TB Alliance connects the best practices and drive of the private sector with the health needs and resources of the public sector. Using a portfolio-driven approach proven by industry, its goal is to develop better anti-TB medicines that will:

- Shorten or simplify TB treatment.
- Be effective against MDR-TB.
- Improve the treatment of latent TB.

The need and market for new antituberculosis drugs

TB infects one-third of the world's population, kills more AIDS patients than any other infection, and costs the global economy $16 billion each year. Since R&D for new TB drugs came to a virtual standstill after the 1960s, TB treatment relies on drugs that are 30–50 years old. Existing anti-TB drugs impose a nine-month treatment regimen that is expensive and cumbersome— slowing down the control of the disease and fuelling the rise of deadly drug resistance.

The TB drug market lacks sufficient incentives to support a pipeline of continually improving drugs. Even with the market potentially reaching $700 million by 2010, it is concentrated in poor countries and no single industry player has pursued the full development of an anti-TB drug. The TB Alliance was designed by the international community as the primary instrument to fill this vacuum and to ensure that new anti-TB drugs are affordable and accessible in TB-endemic countries. This commitment was endorsed by 30 signatories of the February 2000 Cape Town Declaration for TB Drug Development and in the Global Plan to Stop TB.

Drug development via partnerships

The TB Alliance operates like a lean biotechnology firm by building innovative partnerships where risks and incentives are shared. The TB Alliance is stimulating discovery and research, developing a solid portfolio of 20 or more projects, and investing in projects that address infrastructure gaps and help streamline the registration of anti-TB medicines.

While retaining the management oversight of its portfolio projects, the TB Alliance outsources the development of potential drugs to public and private partners via staged funding and expert scientific guidance. The TB Alliance then rigorously supervises its investments though dedicated project management, predefined and measurable milestones, and clear go or no-go decision points and common evaluation criteria.

Paving the way for access

New drugs must be within patients' reach worldwide to ensure affordability, adoption, and patient access to the end product. The TB Alliance will support a drug's development only where it can retain the rights necessary to ensure that the drug will be available, affordable, and accessible. The TB Alliance pursues intellectual property rights through win-win agreements that balance health equity with incentives for collaboration.

A new, faster TB cure will transform global health by accelerating TB treatment and control, overcoming multidrug-resistant strains, and reversing the onslaught of the number one killer of AIDS patients.

Summary of background paper on a two-month drug regimen

The UN Millennium Project Working Group on TB commissioned a study to forecast the potential benefits of a two-month drug regimen for treating tuberculosis (TB). Principal investigators of the study were Dr. Joshua Salomon, Harvard School of Public Health, and Dr. Wayne Getz, University of California, Berkeley.[1] Advisors were Dr. Bartien Borgdorff and Dr. Frank Cobelens of the KNCV Tuberculosis Foundation. This appendix provides details of the resulting paper.

Rationale for modeling project

As the TB epidemic has worsened, the global health agenda has increasingly embraced efforts to develop better TB drugs, diagnostics, and vaccines. In a series of core policy documents, the global TB community emphasizes that better tools will enhance control efforts and accelerate progress toward key targets while strengthening existing DOTS programs. At the onset of a new millennium, beginning as early as the 2000 Amsterdam Ministerial Conference on TB and Sustainable Development, the urgency of accelerated research and development efforts to deliver new drugs, diagnostics, and vaccines has only grown.[2]

Although current TB drugs are recognized for their shortcomings, few forecasts of the likely impact of new drugs that would shorten and simplify TB regimens exist to inform decisionmaking and adjust targets. Since drug regimens are the cornerstone of TB control today, this modeling would help outline the relationship between new technologies, such as faster acting drugs, and current control priorities, such as DOTS expansion. Current drugs are more than 30 years old, impose a lengthy and complex regimen, and necessitate capital-intensive direct patient observation. Today, only one in three patients has access to the proper treatment (DOTS).[3] In this context, would new drugs that require only a two-month instead of a six-month regimen affect patient compliance, cure rates, and case detection? How many cases and deaths could be averted?

This effort is a first attempt to model the benefits of new, faster-acting drugs as a mechanism to support the Millennium Development Goal target of reversing incidence and mortality of TB by 2015. The model approach is a useful aid to public health decisionmaking and resource allocation, since it allows the examination of how a shorter regimen could improve treatment outcomes and reduce transmission. The model exercise can also provide another means to answer key treatment questions in ways that can be more feasible or ethical than clinical trials or observational studies. Models allow for a formal synthesis of information collected from various sources and also highlight unknowns or areas of uncertainty, thereby identifying priorities for further investigation. Critical for the purposes of the UN Millennium Development Project, the modeling approach allows for "what-if" analyses in order to understand possible consequences of different decisionmaking and action.

The multidisciplinary team of modeling and epidemiology experts was coordinated by the Global Alliance for TB Drug Development and overseen by the KNCV Tuberculosis Foundation. The team consists of four investigators at Harvard University, with an expertise in multidrug-resistant tuberculosis (MDR-TB) modeling, and the University of California, Berkeley, with an expertise in TB and HIV. Together they developed a consensus epidemiologic model of TB to forecast the impact of a two-month regimen in treatment programs along three different trajectories: improved compliance, reduced relapse, and enhanced case detection.

The team developed a dynamic core model of TB natural history and epidemiology to predict future trends. This model builds on prior modeling work on TB and key recent studies, including published papers by Chris Dye, World Health Organization (WHO), and Sally Blower, University of California, Los Angeles. This paper outlines the technical aspects, key assumptions, and approach to the TB model constructed to forecast the impact of shorter regimens made possible with new, faster acting drugs.

The basic tuberculosis model

The population is structured into classes describing different states of TB disease and treatment (figure A7.1), broadly divided into susceptibles (S), latent TB infections (IS, IF), active TB cases (AN, AND, AP, APD), cases undergoing treatment (NTD, NTO, PTD, PTO), and partially (RN, RP) or completely (R) recovered individuals. The model is deterministic and operates in discrete timesteps of one month, but within each timestep all processes act as constant per capita rates (using a competing exponential rates formulation).

All individuals are subject to natural mortality at constant per capita rate μ. Individuals who have never been infected with TB occupy the susceptible

Figure A7.1

Schematic of TB treatment model

Note: Mortality rates not shown: All classes suffer natural mortality, μ. Active classes suffer additional mortality, μ_P or μ_N. Treated cases suffer additional mortality, μ_{PD}, μ_{PN}, and so on. S=susceptibles IS, IF = latent TB infections AN, AND, AP, APD = active TB cases NTD, NTO, PTD, PTO = cases undergoing treatment RN, RP = partially recovered individuals R = completely recovered individuals

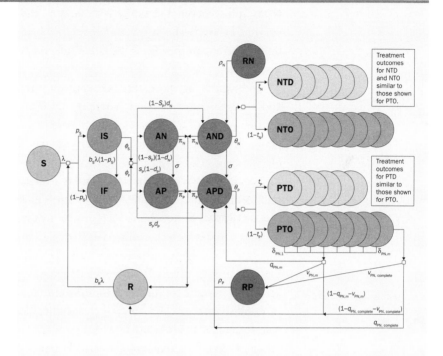

class (S), which is replenished with new recruits based on a specified population fertility rate. Susceptible individuals are infected at rate λ, the force of infection, which is calculated at the beginning of each timestep as described below. A fraction p_S of newly infected individuals enter the latent infection/ slow-progressor class (IS), while the remaining $(1-p_S)$ enter the fast-progressor class (IF). Individuals in IS are subject to reinfection at rate $b_S\lambda$, where b_S is a factor less than one reflecting reduced susceptibility. Of these IS reinfections, only a fraction $(1-p_S)$ move to the IF class, so the net flow from IS to IF is $b_S\lambda(1-p_S)$. Individuals in the IS and IF pools progress to active TB at rates ϕ_S and ϕ_F, respectively, where $\phi_S < \phi_F$.

Active TB cases are divided into four categories, depending on whether they are smear-positive or smear-negative, and whether they are in a detectable or nondetectable pool of the population (where detectability is a function of case-finding effort, geographic location, local health services, and so on). New cases are smear positive with probability s_P or smear negative with probability $(1-s_P)$. A fraction d_P of smear-positive cases are detectable, while for smear-negative cases the fraction is d_N. New active TB cases thus are nondetectable smear positive (AP) and no smear negative (AN) with probabilities $s_P(1-d_P)$ and $(1-s_P)(1-d_N)$, respectively, and detectable smear positive (APD) and smear negative (AND) with probabilities s_Pd_P and $(1-s_P)d_N$. Smear-negative cases convert to smear positive at constant rate σ, with no change in detectability. Smear-positive and smear-negative individuals are subject to additional TB-related mortality at per capita rates μ_P and μ_N, and recover spontaneously to the fully recovered class (R) with rates π_P and π_N. Individuals in the fully recovered class can be infected at rate $b_R\lambda$, where b_R reflects reduced susceptibility, whereupon they enter the latent infection classes as described above for susceptibles.

Individuals in the detectable smear-positive (APD) class are identified and brought onto treatment at rate θ_P. Of individuals entering treatment, a fraction t_P enter DOTS programs while the remainder enter non-DOTS programs. Individuals in DOTS programs are tracked through up to six months of treatment (PTD1–PTD6), and are subject to additional mortality at rate μ_{PD} throughout. Within the mth month of treatment, individuals default (cease treatment) at rate $\delta_{PD,m}$. Defaulters progress to a partially suppressed state of disease (RP) with probability $v_{PD,m}$, revert to active TB (APD) with probability $q_{PD,m}$, or move to the fully recovered (R) class with probability $(1-v_{PD,m}-q_{PD,m})$. Following treatment completion, individuals go to partially suppressed disease (termed "relapse") with probability $v_{PD,complete}$, return immediately to active TB (termed "failure") with probability $q_{PD,complete}$, or recover fully with probability $(1-v_{PD,complete}-q_{PD,complete})$. Individuals with partially suppressed disease are half as infectious as active cases, and reactivate to the APD class at rate ρ_P. Individuals undergoing treatment in non-DOTS programs are tracked through up to eight months of treatment (PTO1–PTO8) and are subject to the same processes as those in DOTS but with different parameters μ_{PN}, $\delta_{PN,m}$, $v_{PN,m}$, and so on. Defaulters and treatment completers who relapse enter the same partially suppressed disease class (RP) as do those relapsing from DOTS. Treatment of smear-negative individuals is set up to run in an analogous manner, with DOTS (NTD1–NTD6) and non-DOTS (NTO1–NTO8) programs and a partially suppressed smear-negative class (RN). All processes are parallel to those described above, with parameters subscripted ND for DOTS and NN for non-DOTS.

The force of infection is calculated for each timestep from the current number of individuals with active disease. The population is assumed to mix randomly, and frequency-dependent incidence (also known as "standard incidence") is employed, reflecting that individuals' contact behavior is not density-dependent. All individuals with untreated smear-positive TB transmit at rate β_P, while those with untreated smear-negative TB transmit at rate β_N. Individuals with partially suppressed smear-positive TB transmit at a fraction of the rate of active cases ($\beta_{RP} = \beta_P/2$). Individuals undergoing DOTS treatment are not infectious ($\beta_{PD} = 0$), while those in non-DOTS programs (with lower drug adherence, on average) transmit at 25 percent the rate of untreated cases ($\beta_{PN} = \beta_P/4$). The overall force of infection at a point in time is thus:

$$\lambda = \frac{\left[\beta_P \left(X_{AP} + X_{APD} \right) + \beta_N \left(X_{AN} + X_{AND} \right) + \beta_{PN} \sum X_{PTO} + \beta_{PN} X_{RP} \right]}{N}$$

where XIJ is the number of individuals in the IJ class, and N is the total size of the modeled population. Note that terms currently set to zero (PTD) or not used (NTD, NTO) are not shown in the above expression.

Extensions to the basic model: multidrug-resistant tuberculosis and tuberculosis and HIV

The core model described above was extended to allow for the development of multidrug-resistant strains through poor treatment and subsequent transmission of resistant strains. We replicated all 42 categories in the model to allow for parallel multidrug-resistant (MDR) and non-MDR states. Development of resistance may occur among those who default from treatment or fail treatment, at a specified probability. Transmission of MDR strains may differ from transmission of non-MDR strains, which we model using a "fitness" parameter.

We also account for the interaction between TB and HIV by replicating all (42 x 2) model states again to allow for two different categories of HIV status: uninfected and infected. Several key natural history parameters vary according to HIV state, including mortality rates, probabilities of developing primary progressive TB within the first few years after infection, and long-term breakdown rates. We also allow for heterogeneous mixing between groups of different HIV status, incorporating an additional parameter that reflects the proportion of contacts for an HIV-infected person who are also HIV-infected, relative to the overall prevalence of HIV infection in the population. HIV incidence is incorporated as an exogenous input to the model, which varies over time to capture relevant trends.

Initial conditions and regional calibration

To calibrate regional models to present conditions in order to examine the potential future impact of new drugs, we ran a series of simulations with parameters representing different phases in TB history. First, a virgin epidemic is simulated, in which one infectious source case in introduced in a population of susceptibles. This epidemic runs to equilibrium, which we assume represents mid-century conditions in many developing regions, prior to the introduction of chemotherapy. We then introduce treatment into the model in stages, reflecting a period of suboptimal treatment and, eventually, expanding coverage of DOTS. Parameters relating to treatment coverage and outcomes were drawn from WHO reports, and calibration to regional epidemiologic data was undertaken in reference to WHO estimates of incidence, prevalence, mortality, and multidrug-resistance prevalence among new cases for the year 2002.

Full list of recommendations from the UN Millennium Project Working Group on TB

The following are the main recommendations proposed by the UN Millennium Project Working Group on TB.

The Millennium Development Goal and its target

- Millennium Development Goal 6 should be amended to read: "Combat HIV/AIDS, malaria, tuberculosis, and other diseases" instead of "Combat HIV/AIDS, malaria, and other diseases."
- In practice, the global tuberculosis (TB) control target should be to halve the prevalence of TB disease and deaths by 2015, to provide a measurable target that is demanding but feasible.

The strategies to achieve the Millennium Development Goal target

- The basic platform for global TB control should remain full implementation of the DOTS strategy. This entails DOTS expansion to engage all primary care providers in delivering the international standard of TB care in line with DOTS, and to ensure that all patients have access to DOTS services. Additional and urgent measures are needed to tackle HIV-related TB and multidrug-resistant tuberculosis (MDR-TB).
- Overall, the focus of activities to meet the Millennium Development Goals target of reversing the incidence of TB and halving TB prevalence and deaths should be on DOTS expansion, addressing TB and HIV/AIDS, mainstreaming DOTS-Plus for MDR-TB, and supporting the development of new diagnostics, new drugs, and new vaccines.
- Success in achieving the target must mean halting the incidence of TB in every region and country of the world, not just on average global figures. This demands a targeted strategy reflecting national characteristics.

The Stop TB Partnership has already established a strategic focus on the 22 countries that together shoulder 80 percent of the global TB burden. Sub-Saharan Africa—which confronts a surge in HIV-related TB cases as well as endemic poverty—must also be a special focus of international support.

Ensure access for all to high-quality tuberculosis care

- All TB patients should have access to the universal standard of care that is based on proper diagnosis, treatment, and reporting consistent with the DOTS strategy. There is urgent need to provide people needing TB diagnosis and treatment with massively expanded access to quality care under DOTS and adapted strategies for HIV-related TB and MDR-TB.

- Bringing these activities to successful outcomes will require long-term commitment from national governments, donors, and the Stop TB Partnership in its broadest sense. The TB community should demonstrate to the donor community and TB-endemic countries the effectiveness and added value of the new Partnership bodies and their products. It should use their initial successes to advocate for sustained support over the next 10 years in order to achieve the Millennium Develoment Goals target by 2015.

- Scaled-up TB control at the national level should build on, and contribute to, improvements in health systems. However, wider action to strengthen health systems in general, and health staffing in particular, will be an imperative. The current weakness of health systems is a major constraint to expanding access to quality TB care.

- Countries should plan to develop systems for routine reporting on TB cases and deaths, and on drug resistance. In the interim, population-based surveys of the prevalence of disease are recommended, especially in countries with high TB or HIV burdens.

Address the tuberculosis and HIV emergency now

- TB and HIV/AIDS partnerships must urgently step up collaboration at the global, national, and service delivery levels to deliver an expanded DOTS strategy to control HIV-related TB. This strategy consists of measures to attack both TB (full implementation of the DOTS strategy with intensified case finding and preventive treatment) and HIV—and therefore indirectly TB—including prevention of HIV transmission and provision of cotrimoxazole and antiretrovirals).

- Countries and donors must focus specific attention on combating the TB and HIV emergency. Tackling the immediate crisis requires an urgent and exceptional effort to maximize the benefit of current levels of funding and support from the international community. Work is now in hand to quantify the increased levels of support needed to meet the Millennium Development Target.

- The expanded DOTS strategy to control HIV-related TB will be successful only through patient-centered, countrywide TB and HIV collaborative service delivery.
- Increased priority must be given to the development of drugs, diagnostics, and vaccines that are reliable in HIV-infected TB patients. This includes drugs that are compatible with antiretroviral treatment.
- Operational research must be intensified to define optimal strategies for joint management of the overlapping epidemics, including effective program collaboration at all levels to mutually improve performance of both TB/HIV programs.

Engage all primary care providers in high-quality tuberculosis care

- Scaled-up TB control should be further integrated as a key component of primary care. TB control depends on effective TB diagnosis, treatment, and follow-up, mainly in primary care.
- National TB programs should engage the full range of public, private, and voluntary healthcare providers in TB control activities under their stewardship, with reform of legislative or regulatory provisions if necessary. The delivery by all providers of care consistent with the DOTS strategy as the internationally recommended standard is crucial to achievement of global TB targets.
- The same high standard of care and support should be provided to all TB patients.
- National TB programs should consider public-private mix approaches as a means to expand and strengthen DOTS, with an emphasis on improving case detection and treatment success.
- TB program managers should seek to include TB control measures in established business sector health activities, especially in HIV/AIDS programs. Government programs in high-burden countries should translate the global guidelines for managing TB at the workplace into local partnership tools to guide collaboration with the employers.

Partner with communities to stop tuberculosis

- National TB programs should intensify efforts to partner with communities in tackling TB and responding to local needs. Potential partners include civil society groups, representatives of TB patients, the broad HIV/AIDS constituency, the local education sector, and local leadership at the grassroots level.
- Donor and technical agencies should support countries in building capacity for advocacy, communications, and social mobilization at all

levels, as part of DOTS expansion plans, and in developing information systems that include indicators on advocacy, communication, and social mobilization. National TB programs should be supported in working with grassroots community groups as an essential part of the strategy to articulate demand for improved healthcare, including TB control.

- National TB programs should work together with grassroots community groups to increase the use of community TB treatment supporters.

Stop the spread of multidrug-resistant tuberculosis

- Prevention of MDR-TB should be tackled through full and effective implementation of DOTS, and treatment via scaled up DOTS-Plus programs, with special urgency in areas where MDR-TB rates are already serious. DOTS-Plus must be mainstreamed into countrywide control plans.
- Investment is needed both to maintain financial support for existing second-line drugs and to develop new drugs. To treat MDR-TB, there needs to be a pipeline of novel drugs, administered in combinations to minimize the emergence of new resistances.
- Urgent support is needed for the Green Light Committee to allow them to provide technical assistance for programs wishing to implement and scale up DOTS-Plus.
- Drug resistance information should be monitored as an indicator of the quality of treatment programs. At the moment, testing TB patients for drug resistance—like testing patients for HIV—tends to be handled as a separate exercise, but the goal should be to incorporate both into routine case surveillance.

Accelerate the development of critically needed new tools

- Donor agencies should increase their investments in the research and development of new and affordable TB diagnostics, drugs, and vaccines through public-private partnerships, and in related projects such as the strengthening of clinical trials capacity in DOTS programs.
- The Stop TB Partnership and the World Health Organization should advocate for these investments to complement their access and treatment efforts. Advocacy should be based on a clear definition of the economic and social justifications of investing in new tools.
- Regulatory agencies should assist in the harmonization of streamlined regulatory requirements for the introduction of new TB diagnostics, drugs, and vaccines.
- The network of Stop TB Partners should work to ensure that new tools respond to the greatest demands of users, and expedite testing and roll-out in high-burden settings.

- Operational research to determine the best ways to implement current interventions, and to monitor their impact, needs to be substantially increased. This requires financial and technical support for national TB programs to enhance local capacity for such research.

Tuberculosis and poverty

- TB partners at all levels should strive for the inclusion of TB in all antipoverty discussions and mechanisms. Most of the high-burden, least-developed, and low-income countries do not include the impact of TB, nor target specific actions to control TB, in their poverty reduction strategies.
- In particular, national TB programs should be encouraged to address the links between TB and poverty in national guidelines and set the agenda politically, for example by advocating for the inclusion of TB control in Poverty Reduction Strategy Papers. They should also welcome partners, such as NGOs, who can assist in providing the poor with services.
- DOTS programs must be flexible enough to meet the needs of patients with special requirements or living in particular conditions or geographic areas, especially the poor and vulnerable. TB partners should continue to innovate in strategies to reach out to them, such as community-based care, social support systems, and public-private models of service delivery.
- DOTS expansion should include equity initiatives in order to ensure that, even among the poor, the less well-off benefit as much as the better-off. DOTS strategy outcome measures should include appropriate indicators.
- Further research is needed to monitor, evaluate, and recommend refined TB control approaches designed to enhance equity and ensure equal access to services.
- Investment in novel R&D efforts to secure new, shorter, and affordable TB diagnosis and treatment is urgently needed to reduce the economic and personal costs to patients, their families, and society as a whole.

Tuberculosis and gender

- On current evidence, in most parts of the world, men face increased risks of TB relative to women, largely due to underlying biological factors and risk of exposure. Still, women fall ill and die due to TB at an alarming level. If we aim to reduce gender differences in development, than we need to address all important gender-related risk factors for disease or poor outcomes.
- As improvement in the welfare and development potential of women, especially in low-income settings, is a high priority, it will be important

to examine underlying factors affecting either very large or very small sex-specific differences in case detection.

- In regions where TB-associated stigma for women is documented, health education and communication programs should urgently address this serious inhibitor to effective treatment and social well being.
- As more information becomes available at the local and national level documenting gender differences in TB disease and access to services, prevention and control strategies should be adapted accordingly. New community-based and public-private service models that aim to increase access and effective treatment, especially for those most vulnerable, should seek to address known gender-related barriers to care.

Tuberculosis and children

- National TB programs should incorporate children with TB in all routine program operations.
- More work should be undertaken on diagnostic algorithms and the study of the epidemiology of childhood TB, especially in low-income settings where the burden is likely to be much higher.
- Operational approaches should be identified to enable health system workers to provide and maintain TB preventive treatment for children.
- The BCG vaccine should continue to be promoted and made available for newborns, as part of the Expanded Program on Immunizations.
- Investment is urgently needed to support the development of new, easy-to-use pediatric anti-TB drug formulations and diagnostic tests, which are effective in infants and children and appropriate for use in resource-poor settings.

Financing needs

- The UN Millennium Project Working Group on TB endorses the recommendation of the WHO Executive Board to the 2005 World Health Assembly, encouraging all countries to fulfill their commitment to ensure the availability of sufficient domestic resources and of sufficient external resources to achieve the 2015 Millennium Development Goal target relevant to TB.
- Updated figures for the resource requirements to achieve the target in line with the recommendations of this report should be provided as part of developing the Global Plan to Stop TB II, 2006–2015. These estimates should be used to advocate for increased levels of funding for TB control and research and development of new tools that are commensurate with the global burden of TB and will provide the full resources needed to reverse this epidemic.
- Adequate GFATM funding and increased GFATM support for TB and TB and HIV efforts needs to be ensured.

- Increased technical support is needed for development and implementation of GFATM-financed projects, as well as programs supported by other sources of finance.
- Additional investment for the private-public research partnerships should be catalyzed, including investment from national governments and other sources.
- It will be important to ensure that funding for TB control becomes more predictable and that any new financing mechanisms, such as the GFATM, are truly additional to existing resources.

Support the Global Plan to Stop TB

- All those involved at global, national, and local levels should come together to invest in the Global Plan to Stop TB, implement its key interventions, and work together to secure its targets: halving TB prevalence and deaths by 2015.
- Ministries of health in countries badly affected by TB should ensure dedicated budget lines for TB control activities and address TB control needs as part of poverty reduction strategies and efforts to strengthen health systems.

Notes

Chapter 1

1. See www.unmillenniumproject.org for detailed history and summary of the UN Millennium Project and its task forces.

2. The United Nations Millennium Declaration can be found at www.unmillenniumproject.org.

3. The first *ad hoc* Committee on the Tuberculosis Epidemic met in 1998, and among other things influenced the establishment of the Partnership and the Global Drug Facility.

Chapter 2

1. The countries are Botswana, Côte d'Ivoire, Djibouti, Kenya, Lesotho, Malawi, Mozambique, Namibia, Somalia, South Africa, Swaziland, Zambia, and Zimbabwe.

2. Unless otherwise shown, data and findings in the section on the overview of the tuberculosis epidemic are taken from WHO (2004j).

3. Unless indicated otherwise, data and findings in the section on MDR-TB are from WHO (2004b, 2004m).

Chapter 5

1. The Global Plan progress report was not able to provide a comprehensive analysis of current investment in tuberculosis control, so an exact assessment of the global tuberculosis funding "gap" was not possible. Based on the fact that the gap identified in the original Global Plan to Stop TB was not filled, while estimated need has increased by some $415 million annually, even without an expanded set of TB/HIV and DOTS expansion costs, the Progress Report estimates an annual funding gap of at least $1 billion for TB control and new tool development.

2. Brazil is not eligible for GFATM funding because of its relatively higher per capita income.

Appendix 2

1. A Gini score of 0 means perfect equality; a score of 100 means perfect inequality.

2. Agencies include the United States Agency for International Development (USAID), John Snow Inc/DELIVER, the U.S. Centers for Disease Control and Prevention (CDC), the World Health Organization (WHO), the Global Drug Facility (GDF), the World Bank, the Royal Dutch TB Association/Canadian International Development Agency, Family Health International/IMPACT, and several other NGOs such as Malteser, Médicins sans Frontières, and a new local NGO funded by Fidelis.

3. The material in this section is taken from NLTP (2003).

4. Williams B., Mansoer J., and Dye C., unpublished data.

5. NLTP (internal database) as reported by Hanson and Mansoer (2003).

Appendix 3

1. www.un.org.kh/who/country.html, accessed 25/7/04.

2. UNDP Human Development Index 2003 and U.S. State Department Cambodia Background Notes: www.state.gov/r/pa/ei/bgn/2732.htm#political.

3. From www.unaids.org/nationalresponse/result.asp. National Response Brief: Cambodia.

Appendix 5

1. Government attempts to improve road conditions have included the establishment of the Ethiopian Rural Travel and Transport Sub-Program.

Appendix 7

1. Other investigators were James Lloyd-Smith, University of California, Berkeley; Megan Murray, Harvard University; Travis Porco, University of California, Berkeley; Steve Resch, Harvard University; Maria Sanchez, University of California, Berkeley; and Milt Weinstein, Harvard University.

2. The increased attention to R&D context has been reaffirmed in the 2001 Global Plan to Stop TB, the 2003 Recommendations of the Ad Hoc Committee to the Stop TB Partnership, and the 2004 Global Plan Update.

3. DOTS is the internationally recommended TB control strategy. It combines five elements, including the use of direct observation of treatment. Once patients with infectious TB have been identified, health and community workers and trained volunteers observe and record patients swallowing the full course of the correct dosage of medicines (treatment lasts six to eight months).

References

Aberra, M., W.M. Kifle, and L. Indrias. 2003. "Child Labor and Associated Problems in a Rural Town in South West Ethiopia." *Ethiopian Journal of Health Development* 17(1): 45–52.

Ad Hoc Committee on the TB Epidemic. 2003. Background document prepared for the meeting of the 2nd Ad Hoc Committee on the TB Epidemic, September 18–19, Montreux, Switzerland.

AMARC Africa. 2003. "The Role of Radio in Educating Communities in TB and HIV/AIDS Health Issues." Paper prepared for the UN Millennium Project Working Group on TB.

Bruchfeld, J., G. Aderaye, I.B. Palme, B. Bjorvatn, S. Ghebremichael, S. Hoffner, and L. Lindquist. 2002. "Molecular Epidemiology and Drug Resistance of Mycobacterium Tuberculosis Isolates from Ethiopian Pulmonary Tuberculosis Patients with and without Human Immunodeficiency Virus Infection." *Journal of Clinical Microbiology* 40(5):1636–43.

Cambodia. 2001. "National Health Strategic Plan for TB Control 2001–2005." Phnom Penh.

———. 2002. "National Poverty Reduction Strategy." Phnom Penh. [Retrieved on November 17, 2004, from www.imf.org/External/NP/prsp/2002/khm/01/].

———. 2003. "Cambodia Millennium Development Goals Report 2003: Challenges and Framework for Action." Phnom Penh.

CMH (Commission on Macroeconomics and Health). 2001. *Macroeconomics and Health: Investing in Health for Economic Development. Report of the Commission on Macroeconomics and Health.* Geneva.

Corbett, E.L., C.J. Watt, N. Walker, D. Maher, B.G. Williams, M.C. Raviglione, and C. Dye. "The Growing Burden of Tuberculosis: Global Trends and Interactions with the HIV Epidemic." *Archives of International Medicine* 163(9):1009–21.

de Jonghe, E., C.J. Murray, H.J. Chum, D.S. Nyangulu, A. Salomao, K. Styblo. 1994. "Cost-Effectiveness of Chemotherapy for Sputum Smear-Positive Pulmonary Tuberculosis in Malawi, Mozambique, and Tanzania." *International Journal of Health Planning and Management* 9(2):151–81.

Demissie, M., H. Getahu, and B. Lindtjorn. 2003. "Community Tuberculosis Care through 'TB Clubs' in Rural North Ethiopia." *Social Science and Medicine* 56(10): 2009–18.

Dolin, P. 1998. "Tuberculosis Epidemiology from a Gender Perspective." In V.K. Diwan, A. Thorson, and A. Winkvist, eds., *Gender and Tuberculosis.* Göteborg, Sweden: Nordic School of Public Health.

Dye, C., and C. Watt. 2004. "The Effect of Tuberculosis Control in China." *Lancet* 364(9432): 417–22.

Elzinga, G., M. Raviglione, and D. Maher. 2004. "Scaling Up: Meeting Targets in Global Tuberculosis Control." *The Lancet* 363(9411): 814–19.

Ethiopia. 1998. "Health Sector Development Programme: Five Year Plan (1990–1994 E.C.)." Ministry of Health, Addis Ababa.

———. 2002. "Ethiopia: Sustainable Development and Poverty Reduction Program." Addis Ababa.

———. 2003a. "Sustainable Development and Poverty Reduction Program Annual Progress Report." Addis Ababa. [www.imf.org/external/pubs/ft/scr/2004/cr0437.pdf].

———. 2003b. "AIDS in Ethiopia." Ministry of Health, Addis Ababa.

Farmer, P., F. Leandre, J. Mukherjee, R. Gupta, L. Tarter, and J.Y. Kim. 2001. "Community-Based Treatment of Advanced HIV Disease: Introducing DOT-HAART (Directly Observed Therapy with Highly Active Antiretroviral Therapy)." *Bulletin of the World Health Organization* 79(12): 1145–51.

Getahun, H., and D. Maher. 2000. "Contribution of 'TB Clubs' to TB Control in a Rural District in Ethiopia." *International Journal of Tuberculosis and Lung Disease* 4(2): 174–78.

GFATM (Global Fund to Fight AIDS, Tuberculosis, and Malaria). 2002. "TB Grant Application: Ethiopia." Geneva. [www.theglobalfund.org/search/docs/1ETHT_524_68_full.pdf].

———. 2003a. "TB Grant Application: Cambodia." Geneva. [www.theglobalfund.org/search/docs/2CAMT_34_0_full.pdf].

———. 2003b. "TB Grant Application: Dominican Republic." Geneva. [www.theglobalfund.org/search/docs/3DMRT_629_0_fullS.pdf].

———. 2004a. "Round 4—Approved Grants." Presentation at the Eighth GFATM Board Meeting, June 28–30, Geneva. [www.theglobalfund.org/en/files/boardmeeting8/round4_sfp.ppt].

———. 2004b. "Global Fund Disbursements." Geneva. [www.theglobalfund.org/en/files/disbursementdetails.pdf].

Gwatkin, D.R. 2003. "How Well Do Health Programs Reach the Poor?" *The Lancet* 361(9357): 540–41.

Hanson C. 2002. "Tuberculosis, Poverty and Inequity: A Review of Literature and Discussion of Issues." Presentation at the Satellite Symposium on TB and Poverty, October 11–12, Montreal, Canada.

Hanson, C., and J. Mansoer. 2003. "Utilization of TB Services in Kenya: An Analysis of Wealth Inequalities." Presentation at the World Bank's Reaching the Poor Conference, February 18–20, Washington, D.C.

Harries, A.D., N.J. Hargreaves, S.M. Graham, C. Mwansambo, P. Kazembe, R. Broadhead, D. Maher, and F.M. Salaniponi. "Childhood Tuberculosis in Malawi: Nationwide Case-Finding and Treatment Outcomes." *International Journal of Tuberculosis and Lung Disease* 6(5): 424–31.

Hudelson, P. 1996. "Gender Differentials in Tuberculosis: The Role of Socio-Economic and Cultural Factors." *International Journal of Tuberculosis and Lung Disease* 77(5): 391–400.

Jha P., O. Bangoura, and K. Ranson. 1998. "The Cost-Effectiveness of Forty Health Interventions in Guinea." *Health Policy and Planning* 13(3): 249–62.

Kangangi, J. K., D. Kibuga, J. Muli, D. Maher, N. Billo, L. N'gang'a, E. Ngugi, and V. Kimani. 2003. "Decentralisation of Tuberculosis Treatment from the Main Hospitals to the Peripheral Health Units and in the Community within Machakos District, Kenya." *International Journal of Tuberculosis and Lung Disease* 7(9, suppl.): S5–S13.

Kenya. 1999. "Report to the Ministry of Health." Health Management Information System, Nairobi.

———. 2000. *Second Report on Poverty in Kenya*. Vol. II of *Poverty and Social Indicators*. Ministry of Finance and Planning, Nairobi.

———. 2002. "Economic Survey 2002." Ministry of Finance and Planning, Central Bureau of Statistics, Nairobi.

———. 2003. "Kenya Demographic and Health Survey 2003: Preliminary Report." Nairobi.

Kimerling, M.E., J. Schuchter, E. Chanthol, T. Kunthy, F. Stuer, P. Glaziou, and O. Ee. 2002. "Prevalence of Pulmonary Tuberculosis among HIV-Infected Patients in a Home Care Program in Phnom-Penh, Cambodia." *International Journal of Tuberculosis and Lung Disease* 6(11): 998–94.

Lönnroth, K., M. Uplekar, V.K. Arora, S. Juvekar, N.T.N. Lan, D. Mvaniki, and V. Pathania. 2004. "Public-Private Mix for Improved TB Control—What Makes It Work?" *Bulletin of the World Health Organization* 82(8): 580–86.

Mao Tan Eang. 2003. "Comprehensive Approach to DOTS Expansion in Cambodia." Presented at the Fourth DOTS Expansion Working Group Meeting, October 7–8, The Hague, Netherlands.

Marseille, E., and L. Garbus. 2002. "Country AIDS Policy Analysis Project: HIV/AIDS in Cambodia." AIDS Policy Research Center, University of California, San Francisco. [http://ari.ucsf.edu/policy/profiles/Cambodia.pdf].

McCoy, S., T. Raftis, N. Varughese, and W. Parks. 2003. "Updates from the Communications, Education, and Behavioral Studies Branch: Stop TB Partnership Advocacy and Communications Assessment of the 22 High-Burden Countries." TB Notes Newsletter 3. [Retrieved on December 2, 2004 from www.cdc.gov/nchstp/tb/notes/TBN_3_03/Upd_comm_edu.htm].

Mitnick, C., J. Bayona, E. Palacios, S. Shin, J. Furin, F. Alcantara, E. Sanchez, M. Sarria, M. Becerra, M.C. Fawzi, M.A. Islam, S. Wakai, N. Ishikawa, A.M. Chowdhury, and J.P. Vaughan. 2002. "Cost-Effectiveness of Community Health Workers in Tuberculosis Control in Bangladesh." *Bulletin of the World Health Organization* 80(6): 445–50.

MSF (Médicins Sans Frontières). 2004. "Running Out of Breath? TB Control in the 21st Century." Campaign for Access to Essential Medicines, Geneva. [www.msf.org/source/annual/tbday/2004/TBDay2004report.doc].

Needham, D.M., P. Godfrey-Faussett, and S.D. Foster. 1998. "Barriers to Tuberculosis Control in Urban Zambia: The Economic Impact and Burden on Patients Prior to Diagnosis." *International Journal of Tuberculosis and Lung Disease* 2(10): 811–17.

Nganda, B., J. Wang'ombe, K. Floyd, and J. Kangangi. 2003. "Cost and Cost-Effectiveness of Increased Community and Primary Care Facility Involvement in Tuberculosis Care in Machakos District, Kenya." *International Journal of Tuberculosis and Lung Disease* 7(9, suppl.): S14–S20.

Nhlema, B., J. Kemp, G. Steenbergen, S. Theobald, S. Tang, and S.B. Squire. 2002. "A Systematic Analysis of TB and Poverty." Report prepared for the TB and Poverty Advisory Committee. Stop TB Partnership, Geneva.

NLTP Kenya (National Leprosy and Tuberculosis Program). 2003a. *National Leprosy and Tuberculosis Program Draft 2003 Annual Report.* Kenya Ministry of Health, Nairobi

———. 2003b. "Informal Survey." U.S. Centers for Disease Control and Prevention, World Bank, and World Health Organization, Nairobi.

NLTP Kenya (National Leprosy and Tuberculosis Program) and KNCV Tuberculosis Foundation. 2004. "Intensified Support and Action Countries (ISAC) Proposal to Stop TB Partnership." Nairobi.

Nunn, P., A. Harries, P. Godfrey-Faussett, R. Gupta, D. Maher, and M. Raviglione. 2002. "The Research Agenda for Improving Health Policy, Systems Performance, and Service Delivery for Tuberculosis Control: A WHO Perspective." *Bulletin of the World Health Organization* 80(6): 471–76.

PAHO (Pan American Health Organization). 2001. "Dominican Republic Profile." Washington, D.C. [Retrieved on July 17, 2004 from www.paho.org/english/sha/prfldor.htm].

PATH (Program for Appropriate Technology in Health). 2000. "Lights of Hope against TB: A National Behavior Change Strategy for Fighting TB in Kenya." IMPACT project funded by the United States Agency for International Development, Seattle, Wash.

PIH (Partners in Health). 2004. "Complex Health Interventions in Poor Settings: Redefining Globalization." Paper presented to International Health Medical Education Consortium Western Regional International Health Conference, Tucson, Ariz.

Rajeswari R., R. Balasubramanian, M. Muniyandi, S. Geetharamani, X. Thresa, and P. Venkatesan. 1999. "Socio-Economic Impact of Tuberculosis on Patients and Family in India." *International Journal of Tuberculosis and Lung Disease* 3(10): 869–77.

RESULTS. 2004. "Integrating HIV/AIDS and TB Efforts: The Challenge for the President's AIDS Initiative." Preliminary report for the U.S. Office of the Global AIDS Coordinator. RESULTS and Open Society Institute, Washington, D.C. [Retrieved on November 17, 2004 from www.results.org/website/download.asp?id=917].

Salaniponi, F., A.D. Harries, T. Nyirenda, A. Banerjee, and D. Nyangulu. 1999. "Putting Research into Policy and Practice: The Experience of the Malawi National Tuberculosis Program." WHO/CDS/CPC/TB 99.268. World Health Organization, Geneva.

Shingadia, D., and V. Novelli. 2003. "Diagnosis and Treatment of Tuberculosis in Children." *The Lancet* 3(10): 624–32.

Stop TB Partnership and WHO (World Health Organization). 2001. "Global Plan to Stop TB 2001–2005." WHO/CDS/STB/2001.16. Geneva.

———. 2003. "Public-Private Mix for DOTS: Practical Tools to Help Implementation, TB Strategy and Operations." WHO/CDS/TB/2003.325. Geneva.

———. 2004a. "Background Document Prepared for the Meeting of the 2nd Ad Hoc Committee on the TB Epidemic." Geneva.

———. 2004b. "Recommendations to Stop TB Partners." Paper presented at the meeting of the 2nd Ad Hoc Committee on the TB Epidemic. Geneva.

———. 2004c. "Progress Report on the First Global Plan to Stop TB." WHO/HTM/STB/2004.29. Geneva. [www.stoptb.org/documents/progress_report_2004.pdf].

Styblo, K., and H.J. Chum. 1987. "Treatment Results of Smear-Positive Tuberculosis in the Tanzania National Tuberculosis and Leprosy Program: Standard and Short-Course Chemotherapy." In *Proceedings of the XXVI IUAT World Conference on Tuberculosis and Respiratory Diseases.* Tokyo: Professional Postgraduate Services.

Sykes, M., R. Tolhurst, and S.B. Squire. 2003. "Vulnerable Patients and the Public-Private Mix in Tuberculosis." Background paper for the *Report on Tuberculosis of the Task Force on HIV/AIDS, Malaria, Tuberculosis, and Access to Essential Medicines.* UN Millennium Project, New York.

UN (United Nations). 2002. "United Nations Population Division, World Population Prospects, 2002 Revision." [Retrieved on September 13, 2004, from http://esa.un.org/unpp/sources.html].

———. 2000. "Country Health Information Profile: Cambodia." [Retrieved on July 25, 2004 from www.un.org.kh/who/country.html].

UNAIDS (Joint United Nations Programme on HIV/AIDS). 2002. "Country Profile: Dominican Republic" [Retrieved on July 7, 2004 from www.unaids.org/en/geographical+area/by+country/dominican+republic.asp/].

———. 2004 "National Response Brief: Cambodia." [Retrieved December 2, 2004 from www.unaids.org/nationalresponse/result.asp].

UNDP (United Nations Development Programme). 2003. *Human Development Report 2003: Millennium Development Goals: A Compact among Nations to End Human Poverty.* New York: Oxford University Press.

UN Millennium Project. 2004. "Millennium Development Goals Needs Assessment: Background Paper to 'Ending Africa's Poverty Trap.'" Working paper. New York. [www.unmillenniumproject.org/html/backgroundpaper.shtm].

———. 2005. *Investing in Development: A Practical Plan to Achieve the Millennium Development Goals.* London: Earthscan.

USAID (United States Agency for International Development). 2003. "USAID Development Experience Clearinghouse." Washington, D.C. [Retrieved on September 13, 2004 from www.eldis.org/static/DOC14620.htm].

U.S. Department of State. 2003. "Cambodia Background Notes." Washington, D.C. [Retrieved on July 15, 2004 from www.state.gov/r/pa/ei/bgn/2732.htm#political].

Van der Linde, M. 2003. "Grassroots-level Advocacy and Social Mobilization for TB: A Peruvian Experience." Presented at The Experts' Consultation on Communications and Social Mobilization in Support of the Global Plan to Stop TB. June 29–July 1, Cancún.

WHO (World Health Organization). 1997. "New Report Confirms Global Spread of Drug-Resistant Tuberculosis: 'Hot Zones' Identified by Scientists Outbreaks Linked to Poor Control." Press Release. [Retrieved on November 17, 2004 from www.who.int/archives/inf-pr-1997/en/pr97-74.html].

———. 2001a. "Good Practice in Legislation and Regulations for TB Control: An Indicator of Political Will." WHO/CDS/TB/2001.290. Geneva.

———. 2001b. "Global DOTS Expansion Plan—Progress in TB Control in High-Burden Countries 2001: 1 year after the Amsterdam." Geneva.

———. 2001c. "Macroeconomics and Health: Investing in Health for Economic Development." Report of the Commission on Macroeconomics and Health. Geneva. [Retrieved on August 9, 2004, from www.cmhealth.org/].

———. 2001d. "Ministerial Conference." WHO/CDS/STB/2001.11. Geneva.

———. 2002a. "Strategic Framework to Decrease the Burden of TB/HIV." WHO/CDS/TB/2002.296, WHO/HIV_AIDS/2002.2. Geneva.

———. 2002b. "Report on DOTS Expansion Working Group Meeting, Montreal, Canada." Internal document. Geneva.

———. 2002c. *The Economic Impacts of Tuberculosis.* Stop TB Initiative 2000 Series. WHO/CDS/STB/2000.5. Geneva.

———. 2002d. *WHO Report on Infectious Diseases 2002: Scaling Up the Response to Infectious Disease.* Geneva

————. 2003a. *Scaling UP Antiretroviral Therapy in Resource-Limited Settings: Treatment Guidelines for a Public Health Approach*, rev. ed. Geneva.

————. 2003b. "Community Contribution to Care: Practice and Policy." WHO/CDS/TB/2003.312. Geneva.

————. 2003c. "Treatment of Tuberculosis: Guidelines for National Programs." WHO/CDS/TB 2003.313. Geneva.

————. 2003d. "Country Atlas." [Retrieved December 15, 2004 from www.int/global/dataQuery/viewdata.asp].

————. 2004a. "Interim Policy on Collaborative TB/HIV Activities." WHO/HTM/TB/2004.330. Geneva.

————. 2004b. *Anti-Tuberculosis Drug Resistance in the World*. Prevalence and Trends Report 3. Geneva.

————. 2004c. "Strategic Framework to Decrease the Burden of TB/HIV." WHO/CDS/TB/2002.296, WHO/HIV_AIDS/2002.2. Geneva.

————. 2004d. "Guidelines for HIV Surveillance among Tuberculosis Patients." WHO/HTM/2004.339, WHO/HIV/2004.06, UNAIDS/04.30E. Geneva.

————. 2004e. *World Health Report 2004: Changing History*. Geneva.

————. 2004f. *PRSPs: Their Significance for Health: Second Synthesis Report*. Geneva.

————. 2004g. "DOTS for All: Country Reports." Regional Office for the Western Pacific, Manila

————. 2004h. *Global TB Report. Country Case Study: Cambodia*. Geneva.

————. 2004i. *Global TB Report. Country Case Study: Ethiopia*. Geneva.

————. 2004j. *Global Tuberculosis Control: Surveillance, Planning, Financing*. Geneva.

————. 2004k. "Meeting Report of Core Group Meeting." Global TB/HIV Working Group. Geneva. [www.who.int/gtb/5thcoregroupmtg_feb04/finalreport.doc].

————. 2004l. "Gender and Tuberculosis." Department of Gender, Women and Health, Geneva. [www.who.int/gender/documents/en/TB.factsheet.pdf].

————. 2004m. "Drug Resistant TB Ten Times Higher in Eastern Europe and Central Asia." Press Statement, March 16. Geneva.

————. 2004n. "DOTS" [Retrieved on December 2, 2004, from www.who.int/tb/dots/whatisdots/en/].

————. 2004o. *"Sustainable Financing for Tuberculosis Control."* Resolution of the Executive Board. EB114.R1, 14th session, May 25, Geneva.

WHO (World Health Organization) and ILO (International Labour Organization). 2003. "Guidelines for Workplace TB Control Activities." WHO/CDS/TB/2003.323. Geneva.

WHO (World Health Organization) and Stop TB Partnership. 2001. "Towards a TB-Free Future." WHO/CDS/STB/2001.13. Geneva.

WHO (World Health Organization), CDC (U.S. Centers for Disease Control and Prevention), IUALTD (International Union against Tuberculosis and Lung Disease), and USAID (United States Agency for International Development). 1997. *Anti-Tuberculosis Drug Resistance in the World*. Geneva.

Wilkinson, D. 1999. "Eight Years of Tuberculosis Research in Hlabisa—What Have We Learned?" *South African Medical Journal* 89(2):155–59.

Wilkinson, D., and G.R. Davies. 1997. "Coping with Africa's Increasing Tuberculosis Burden: Are Community Supervisors an Essential Component of the DOT Strategy? Directly Observed Therapy." *Tropical Medicine and International Health* 2 (7): 700–04.

World Bank. 1993. *World Development Report 1993: Sustainable Development in a Dynamic World: Transforming Institutions, Growth and Quality of Life*. New York: Oxford University Press.

———. 2001. "Socio-Economic Differences in Health, Nutrition, and Population: Kenya." Washington, D.C.

———. 2004. World Development Indicators Database. [Retrieved on September 13, 2004 from http://devdata.worldbank.org.ezp2.harvard.edu/dataonline/].